AF687991

ALGORITHMIC DUTY OF CARE

Front Cover Image By Daniel Eskridge

Artist Description: Lady Justice/Themis/Justitia is the representation of morality in governing and law. She's about doing the right thing over just doing the legal thing. In some ways she represents a rebellious notion that while governments can decide what is allowed and what is not, they cannot change what is right and what is wrong.

ALGORITHMIC DUTY OF CARE

Algorithm—Love Thy Neighbor

A New Social Contract for the Age of Algorithms

ALGORITHMIC DUTY OF CARE

First Edition

Dr. Cindy Mason
Mr. Curt Hall

Berkeley, California
May, 2025

Copyright 2025 Cindy Mason and Curt Hall
First Edition 2025
San Francisco, California

ISBN: 979-8-9904750-0-7 (Soft Cover)
ISBN: 979-8-9904750-1-4 (Hard Cover)

Library of Congress Control Number: 2025908296
Algorithmic Duty of Care
by Dr. Cindy Mason and Mr. Curt Hall
Cover Image Art by Daniel Eskridge
Outer Cover Design: Cindy Mason
Book Creation: Cindy Mason

This is a companion book to *Artificial Compassion Technology Design* and *The Emotion Organon.*

All rights reserved. No part of this publication may be reproduced, stored in a retrieval system, or transmitted, in any form or by any means, electronic, mechanical, photocopying, recording or otherwise, without the prior permission of the authors.

All inquiries should be sent to cmason@cmason.us

Thanks

Thanks to Robert Cook, PhD, Elizabeth Morrow, PhD, Anne Twomey, JD, Bill Fenwick, JD(RIP), Sir Tony Nolan, JP, Henry Lieberman, PhD, Nelson Max, Richard Waldinger, PhD, the SRI AI Coffee Group, Emily Hall, Paul Harmon.

Duty of Care is Ancient and Universal

The principle of neighborly care is a universal ethical idea, though expressed differently depending on culture or scripture, as the quotes from religions around the world show (below). They reveal that care is a powerful and universal human instinct that can transcend religious or national boundaries—making it a strong foundation for cross-cultural approaches to things like algorithmic responsibility.

Judaism
"You shall love your neighbor as yourself."

—Leviticus 19:18 (Tanakh)

Christianity
"Love your neighbor as yourself. There is no commandment greater than these."

—Mark 12:31 (New Testament)

Islam
"He is not a believer who eats his fill while his neighbor goes hungry."

—Hadith, Sahih al-Bukhari

Hinduism
"This is the sum of duty: do not do to others what would cause pain if done to you."

—Mahabharata 5:1517

(An early formulation of the "Golden Rule," connected to neighborly ethics.)

Buddhism
"As a mother would protect her only child, even at the risk of her own life, so should one cultivate a boundless love toward all beings."

—Metta Sutta (Sutta Nipāta 1.8)

Confucianism
"Never impose on others what you would not choose for yourself."

—Analects 15:24

We are creating algorithms to make decisions for us and to be a part of our lives. The duty of care also belongs in our algorithms.

NOTES TO THE READER

Cindy Mason, CMT, PHD
Former Fellow, Stanford School of Medicine

This book isn't a silver bullet—it's a beginning. I've been working in AI for more than 20 years at places like U.C. Berkeley, NASA and Stanford University. For much of that time I have been working at the intersection of software agents and emotion science. Lately, I've been building a data set involving faces of compassion, and working on a book about Artificial Compassion—which involves not just AI but virtual reality, video games, and other technologies. So believe me when I tell you that the last thing I thought I would be doing right now is writing a book about law, caring and algorithms. The short version of why I wrote this book is that I have slowly grown to see that law is not only about control, it is about care. I wrote this book because I realized that in the mad rush to create all kinds of amazing new technology, we are leaving out something important to people: caring.

People care about each other. It's actually so important to us that its all around us. It's a big part of being human and staying alive, especially when you are vulnerable. It's why we cheer for underdogs, cry at rescue stories, and share videos of kindness. Caring is everywhere—except in our algorithms. It is important to remember that we are not just the users of these algorithms and models, we are their authors and inventors. We can create a new kind of technology and a new technical culture—one involving an algorithmic duty of care. It's a world we can inhabit for a long time.

My awareness of this need to create a new paradigm for computing came while I was doing research on the Artificial Compassion book. I came across something that happened in Australia involving an algorithm called Robodebt. The Robodebt algorithm left a trail of devastation and took years to unravel. Many people suffered and some died.

A one-off, I thought. Surely an isolated incident. But then I discovered another algorithmic scandal in the U.K.: the Horizon IT postal scandal. It's an ongoing case—the criminal trial begins in 2027. The harm caused by this algorithm (and by the people who looked the other way) was also devastating. Innocent people, wrongly accused, lost their homes, jobs, families, communities, and futures. Some went to jail. Some turned to drugs and alcohol. And it has taken decades to unravel. Another isolated incident? I thought so. But then I discovered more. These are the situations we were warned about by Joy Boulamwini at MIT and in Cathy O'Neil's book, Weapons of Math Destruction. But now it's happening.

What makes this present situation even more acute is that at the same time that these algorithmic scandals were brewing, there was a renaissance in medical science around human emotion. It is perhaps even more remarkable than what's happening with AI. One key discovery is that more than 50% of our bodily processes, cells, and organ functions depend on the biological effects of positive emotions like compassion. Another important discovery relates to *bioplasticity*—a process by which we physically change in response to the people, places, and things we spend time with.

Bioplasticity is not limited to the brain or immune system, as was once imagined. It has been measured in many other systems, including our genes and the heart. This is really important if you consider that heart disease is the number one killer worldwide. Although this was happening in medicine, this spoke to me as a computer scientist. I realized that while the world fixates on AI as a technological marvel, and our lives are increasingly shaped by machines (and the people who control them) we are also experiencing something more profound. According to bioplasticity, we are being changed by our experiences—good and bad. We need to change how we're designing technology. Because technology rubs off on us: we now co-inhabit a world with technology and algorithms that impact us.

In effect, our designs need to be compatible with these discoveries. If we are going to create technology that aligns with our biology, then tech culture also needs to align with these discoveries. Our technologies need to have a stake in us—to care about us. We need a new paradigm. But that's not all. This gap of care between people and algorithms is widening, as more areas of our life are governed by algorithms. That observation is even more troubling than the algorithmic scandals themselves. But I also see hope.

What you find when you look beyond the fear and the headlines is that some people are working on solutions. They are already designing care and compassion into technology. Crucially, the law is beginning to catch up to the algorithmic harm. Around the globe, legal systems are responding to the new reality we share with algorithms and devices. Landmark cases—like *Ethiopia vs Meta*—are redefining the boundaries of corporate responsibility. New laws are being drafted from Brussels to Brasília. A global legal landscape is emerging—but we're building it in the middle of a storm.

This book is a map of that new legal terrain. It touches on our historical struggles with care, law, and power—from foundational frameworks like the Magna Carta and the birth of common law to the present-day ethical and legal crises brought about by algorithmic harm. And it explores a worldwide response that's giving rise to a new kind of accountability—one centered on caring.

The book also looks ahead—to the future we're creating through emerging laws that are still works in progress. These range from updates to employment law to bold proposals like an AI Bill of Rights, and even the development of AI systems that are creating and interpreting law.

—Cindy 5.4.25

Mr. Curt Hall
Emerging Technologies Analyst

There has never been a more urgent time to advocate for an Algorithmic Duty of Care. As I write this, 45 grieving families whose children were harmed by social media are protesting in front of Meta's corporate New York City headquarters, demanding the company institute better safeguards for kids within its social media platforms. This includes presenting a formal letter, signed by over 10,000 people (!), including prominent online safety groups, urging Meta's leadership to implement meaningful changes to its Facebook and Instagram digital properties.

This moment, poignant as it is, reflects only one facet of a larger, more profound narrative. While the societal impact of social media is undeniably vast, the reach of algorithms actually extends far beyond social platforms and even our screens: algorithms now weave themselves into the very fabric of our lives—shaping education, finance, healthcare, employment, entertainment, and even our justice system. Simply put, the "algorithmification" of society is happening at a breakneck pace, and its implications demand our full attention. Now.

Today, more than ever, we don't simply "use" computer programs; we live within them. When it comes to gaming, social media, virtual reality and forms of entertainment, our lives have become immersed in digital worlds, with users spending many hours daily deeply engaged by their features and functionality. Yet such digital environments influence not just our time, but our decisions and experiences as well. In short, algorithms are not mere tools—they are architects of the digital spaces in which we reside. They exert a significant influence on the lives of billions of people every day: some directly as end users of digital programs; others, more indirectly—such as job applicants having their interviews recorded and analyzed by AI systems working behind the scenes to gauge their potential for meeting job requirements.

But this is really just the beginning. As an information technology analyst who has covered the development of emerging technologies for more than 20 years, I believe we are on the brink of a profound digital revolution—one where algorithms reshape society at an unprecedented scale. With each AI advancement, these systems grow more pervasive, making decisions of immense consequence and removing human oversight from the loop. And as AI continues to evolve at a stunning rate, organizations will increasingly use AI (itself) to design even more advanced AI systems, accelerating a future where algorithms hold sway over practically every aspect of our lives.

With such trust comes risk, and when algorithms falter the repercussions can be devastating: the qualified woman doesn't get the job; the clerk is wrongly accused of stealing; the minority gets a harsher prison sentence or is denied parole; the social security recipient is wrongly accused of fraud; and the family has their children taken away. What should happen when algorithms make mistakes? Who bears responsibility for the harm? And beyond accountability, what obligation do these systems—and the people overseeing them—have to actively prevent foreseeable harm?

This is where Algorithmic Duty of Care enters the conversation. Drawing on the bedrock legal and ethical principle of "duty of care"—the obligation to act responsibly to avoid causing harm—this concept expands the idea to the realm of algorithms. An Algorithmic Duty of Care establishes a foundation for accountability, responsibility, and prevention within our digital environments. It emphasizes proactive measures over reactive remedies, providing a roadmap for mitigating harm before it occurs.

The bottom line is simple yet profound: care matters. It is a cornerstone of our humanity, reflected in the relationships we nurture and the communities we build. As algorithms increasingly shape our world, isn't it time we extend that same principle of care to them?

—Curt 4.30.25

A MAP OF THE BOOK

Part I

Chapter 1: Introduction—Introduces the concept of duty of care and the universally upheld social norm of love thy neighbor. These concepts are more important now than ever because the algorithmification of the world is underway and the idea of caring for people is not part of it. The Magna Carta can help. Contains narrative guide and overall book organization.

Chapter 2: Algorithms and The Magna Carta—The Magna Carta is still relevant today: the new digital "kingdoms" have more people than most countries. Duty of care is everywhere except in our algorithms. Explore how the Magna Carta can help today as we invent algorithmic worlds.

Chapter 3: Algorithmic and Data Duty of Care—Reveals three current cases of algorithmic disaster: Horizon IT, Dutch childcare benefits scandal and Robodebt. A widening gap has emerged between the direction our algorithms are taking us and these breakthroughs in medical science. People make bad guardrails, justice is slow, but if we add a technology component, we move from reacting to preventing.

Chapter 4: Algorithms and Social Power—The world has changed—we invented something to make our decisions for us. But we need more than that—it needs to reflect our values.

Chapter 5: ADOC Defined—Algorithmification of government and the global response to harm.

Chapter 6: Crisis Driven Regulation—Explores current legal cases and new avenues of law and government to face the challenges.

Part II

Chapters 7-16: Algorithms and Evolving Law—Each chapter explores key elements of algorithmic policies and legislations happening in different countries around the world.

Appendix

Parting Words

Glossary

Table of Contents

PART I

Algorithms, Duty of Care and the Law

CHAPTER 1

INTRODUCTION

In this book, we introduce the concept of an Algorithmic Duty of Care (ADOC). Computer codes, or algorithms, are now taking on roles and making decisions once reserved for people. This process, which we call *algorithmification*, is happening rapidly with profound and often invisible consequences. Across the globe, algorithms are increasingly shaping the decisions that affect our lives in a wide range of places including government, education, healthcare, communication, news, and more. They are increasingly becoming the invisible force behind many aspects of our personal daily life, including our professions.

Crucially, many of these systems are being designed and deployed without any embedded duty of care. The result is a growing series of algorithmic disasters and wrongly upended lives. In response, legal frameworks and cultures around the world are scrambling to respond to this situation and they are catching up fast. You will learn about this here in the book.

You will also learn that there's a better way to build technology than mere knee jerk reactions to disasters. We need an algorithmic strategy that has a stake in us—a strategy that cares about us: Algorithmic Duty of Care.

Algorithm, Love Thy Neighbor

The duty to care for our neighbors is possibly as old as humankind. It appears in religious and philosophical traditions around the world in various forms—from the Bible and the teachings of Confucius to Hinduism, Judaism, Islam, and others. It's also a foundational principle in law. But when it comes to human-made algorithms, things are different. These systems aren't people—they're machines, mostly made by corporations and their employees, who follow their own internal rules. For example, in the United States, a corporation's duty of care is primarily to its shareholders. The algorithmic scandals we are experiencing today show us that the people who oversee them (the algorithms) may not be governed by any clear standards of accountability.

ADOC offers a forward-looking strategy. Instead of relying solely on a patchwork of reactive responses (and lawsuits) to algorithmic disasters, it proposes that we also work to prevent them—by extending the neighborly and legal concept of a duty of care to the algorithms that shape our lives. Though rooted in long-standing legal and ethical traditions, this duty of care can also be written into code.

Today the world's attention is on AI—and while an AI duty of care makes sense, this isn't just an AI problem. It's an algorithmic one. Unlike many books on technology and ethics, this one is grounded in three real-world cases where the lack of care in algorithmic design caused measurable harm: Horizon IT in the United Kingdom, Robodebt in Australia, and Toeslagenaffaire, the childcare benefits scandal, in the Netherlands. Each of these disasters unfolded differently, but they share a common thread: institutions and oversight systems were in place, but they failed—ending and devastating lives in the process.

How do we go about creating an *algorithmic* duty of care? Fortunately, the concept of *duty of care* already exists globally, and it has a strong legal and cultural foundation. In 1215, a document was written—not merely ink on parchment, but a legal foundation, a framework that would reach across centuries. Today, its ideas are reflected in the constitutions and bills of rights of nations spanning the globe, shaping law, governance, human dignity and the very idea of justice. The ideas in this document can be very helpful to us in laying a foundation for ADOC—Algorithmic Duty of Care.

Like the core ideas of today's algorithmic systems, the Magna Carta crossed borders. It was born of the need to restrain power and protect the humanity of individuals. We describe these ideas here in this book. In Part II of the book you will find a global summary of the laws, policies and regulations cropping up around the world. They serve as evidence of our inherent caring nature.

When the Dog Rescues the Baby Deer

Duty of care is a social, ethical, and legal principle that refers to the obligation of individuals or organizations to act with reasonable care in ways that avoid foreseeably causing harm to others—that is, to act responsibly. This notion of caring and responsibility is not limited to a specific culture or country, or even just to humans. If you've ever watched animal videos on the internet—perhaps one showing a dog rescuing a baby deer from a pit, or a dolphin guiding a stranded whale back to the sea—you can recognize that even in animals, an instinctive duty of care exists. These videos often go viral, a testament to how deeply rooted this ethic is in all of us. Duty of care is so intrinsic to our humanity that it's evident everywhere—except in one area: the algorithms we are building.

Algorithmification and Oblivatronix Systems

This is important to notice because we are in the midst of "algorithmifying" much of human life and society. Algorithmification—its when computational algorithms are used to set standards, monitor human activities, and influence human behavior. From everyday services such as banking and shopping to the algorithmification of professional practices and institutions, this transformation is reshaping education, healthcare, culture, social services and business. Central to the social, cultural and communication shift is what we call "platformification"—a process in which a small group of global corporations, primarily based in the United States, create algorithms called platforms that allow content to be uploaded and delivered across vast networks. These platforms are as influential as the video game industry and have significant influence on culture and communication worldwide. In all of these sectors, the focus has often been on developing applications that can "just do the job" without considering the broader implications for human vulnerability. These systems are *oblivious* to us as vulnerable human beings. We call this the "Oblivatronix generation" of technology.

This brings us to some important questions: If duty of care is so fundamental to us, why haven't we been including it in our algorithms? But the more pressing question is *what can we do about it now?* The answer introduced here is to establish an Algorithmic Duty of Care, one that brings the same duty of care we see in the world around us to our algorithms, data systems, and the people who oversee them. You will see how much this matters to people in the steady rise of laws being shaped across countries and cultures summarized in the chapters in Part II of this book.

There is a duty of care (responsibility framework) that applies to everything else humans create—houses, transportation, medication, institutional practices, not to mention safeguarding responsibilities for nearly all human to human encounters. Because our digital systems are shaping so much of society, it is common sense that we open ourselves to this way of thinking about our designs. And that we design systems to design themselves this way as well (e.g. machine learning systems, automatic code generators, etc.).

As with duty of care in the physical world, we need to foster awareness of its importance in digital spaces—especially in areas, both physical and digital, where it's lacking or where people are oblivious to its significance to life. In the U.S., for example, corporations prioritize a duty of care not to the public, but to their shareholders. While it's a nice idea to hope that this might change, it's unlikely to happen in the near future. For CEOs, it's crucial to demonstrate that ADOC isn't just the right thing to do—it's also beneficial for their bottom line, as we will show in the following pages. Practically speaking, to implement ADOC, we need a technical understanding of how to design these systems and a legal framework to ensure their proper oversight. Together these may guide or support human oversight.

From Kings to Code

The idea that power must be accountable didn't begin with modern democracy. It has deep roots in legal history, particularly in England's transformation after the Norman Conquest of 1066. When William the Conqueror defeated King Harold at the Battle of Hastings and claimed the English throne, he didn't just change the monarchy—he began to reshape the entire legal system.

Under William's successors, especially Henry II in the 12th century, a new kind of justice emerged: common law. Unlike local or tribal customs, common law created a unified legal framework based on *precedent*—what judges had decided in previous cases. It was one of the earliest systems where law began to bind the rulers as well as the ruled.

Then came the Magna Carta in 1215—a revolutionary document where barons forced King John to recognize that even the monarch was not above the law. At its core, the Magna Carta was about duty, restraint, and care: if you held power, you had a responsibility not to use it arbitrarily or harmfully. That principle—an early form of *duty of care*—has echoed through centuries of legal thinking.

Today, we are undergoing another transformation. Algorithms are the new agents of power. They don't wear crowns or ride into battle—but they decide who gets a loan, who gets investigated, who gets overlooked. Their influence is vast, often invisible, and largely unregulated.

As we look for ways to build Algorithmic Duty of Care, we don't have to start from scratch. We can draw from the bedrock of legal foundations laid in moments like the Norman Conquest and the signing of the Magna Carta—times when societies realized that power, whether held by kings or code, must answer to something greater than itself: *the people it affects.*

ADOC and The Magna Carta

The inspiration for ADOC comes from the universal human (and animal) instinct to care for one another, common law, and the Magna Carta. As previously described, it is a cornerstone document that formalized duty of care and inspired or founded constitutions and legal protections now found throughout the modern world. Some of its most famous achievements include the rule of law and the idea that even those in the highest levels of power—such as a King—are subject to the rule of law. This is why it is an inspiration for ADOC. You will see much discussion in this book about duty of care, the Magna Carta, and ADOC.

The need for an Algorithmic Duty of Care as part of a regulatory, corporate, or social responsibility framework is critical. As you read this, efforts to develop such frameworks and policies are underway in many countries around the world. However, in the United States, federal regulations on this front have been scaled back or eliminated. This makes the ideas in this book especially important for the U.S.; the "algorithmification" of our world is a path we have never walked before—much like a journey to Mars. In this book we also look at the cases of the Horizon IT Postal scandal, Robodebt, and Toeslagenaffaire, the dutch childcare benefits scandal—three algorithmic disasters that represent prior knowledge and experience that the U.S., and many other nations, can learn from. These cases demonstrate what is at stake right now. They also show how flawed algorithms can sometimes cause significant harm to individuals, families, corporations and society at large.

Economic Rationale

For corporations, embedding care isn't just moral—it also avoids costly scandals, lawsuits, and reputational harm. What's vital to understand right now is this: the "oblivatronix" nature of many algorithms is not only upending lives but also driving enormous costs, as investigations and legal battles evolve into full-blown algorithmic scandals. Not only can such cases drag on for many years, during that slow resolution process, the harm caused by these broken systems continues to unfold like a slow-motion train wreck. One of the key advantages of designing algorithms and data systems with a duty of care is that it helps prevent such harm before it occurs, offering a proactive solution to an otherwise reactive system. This is crucial because we live in a world where we are continuously introducing algorithms and data systems that not only expand in scope and reach, but now touch the most sensitive areas of our lives—our jobs, bank loans, court decisions, and more.

Duty of care isn't just about the algorithms themselves; it also pertains to the people who looked the other way while overseeing these systems. This is why the concept of ADOC needs to be part of the public conscience, and why we require both a legal and technical framework.

The United Kingdom's Horizon IT accounting algorithm scandal has spanned a quarter of a century, and it's not even finished yet—the criminal trial is expected to *begin in 2027*. The people in charge of Horizon IT ignored user complaints as well as expert advisors, leading to great human suffering and death. The damage caused by this particular algorithm was limited to the U.K. But this is not always the case.

Lines Across a Borderless Map

When algorithms are developed by global or multi-national corporations, their algorithms—and the values underlying them—are often 'exported' to other countries, leading to potential clashes between differing cultures of care, government policies and legal systems.

For example, in the U.S., corporate duty of care is primarily focused on shareholders, and this approach to algorithm design is being exported through platforms and applications to countries where the duty of care also includes public welfare. Additionally, the U.S. has a unique perspective on freedom of speech, which influences how a U.S. company responds to user complaints about content posted on platforms (that are run by algorithms). When these differing cultures of care collide, the result is often human harm and legal disputes. A current example of this is the ongoing dispute between Ethiopia and Meta. This is discussed in detail in Chapter 6. But the issue could not be more real—Ethiopian plaintiffs are asking for $2.4 billion (£1.8 billion) and for Meta to change their algorithms (1). It's not just about money, either. People died (2).

This is just one of the many class action lawsuits involving duty of care that you learn about here. They are taking years of litigation and costing billions in settlement and legal fees. Clearly, it's better for a company's bottom line and reputation to avoid scandals, expenses, and court cases from the outset. Algorithmic Duty of Care can be integrated into systems in simple, practical ways—making it a reasonable and essential next step in the evolution of algorithms, especially for those responsible for designing or overseeing these systems.

From a consumer's point of view, we find ourselves without an Algorithmic Duty of Care as more and more algorithms emerge in the world. Exporting the ideas of the Magna Carta to such new digital kingdoms through frameworks like the Algorithmic Duty of Care is important for consumers. This is not just for sentimental reasons or because the world revolves around people caring about each other, but because there have already been serious tragedies.

The purpose of this book is to inspire people to think about what it means for algorithms and duty of care to come together, and to take actions before more algorithmic disasters occur. It is not enough to have human oversight and legal frameworks. I'm not the only one to recognize this; the design, development and deployment of Post-Oblivatronix technology is already happening in a wide range of applications. To learn more about this see *Artificial Compassion Technology Design* (3).

We have a choice now: spend decades enduring investigations and lengthy court cases while people continue to suffer, which is what is happening, or embed frameworks and policies into our technologies and legalities that will provide a proactive approach. We need to learn from what has already happened. In fact, as you will see in Part II, many countries, states and cities are not only learning from what has happened they are already hard at work creating laws that will result in a culture of algorithmic duty of care.

Part I & II—A Narrative Bridge

At this juncture in time, you could say we're standing on a kind of threshold. One foot in the world as it has long been, the other stepping into something unfamiliar —something made, not grown. The world of algorithms is not a new continent or a new century. It is something stranger: a new kind of governance, a lattice of decisions made without pause, without sleep, and often, without accountability.

Some of the people alive today—perhaps your children, or theirs—will grow up never knowing a world before this one. A world where decisions were made by people you could see, laws you could argue, systems you could name. Before algorithms whispered verdicts through loan applications, job screenings, border checks, and welfare audits.

Before something as vast and quiet as a statistical model could determine the shape of a life.

We have built this world ourselves—line by line, model by model—but mostly without the benefit of what we've learned the hard way over centuries: that unchecked power tends to go badly; that fairness needs rules; that harm, if not anticipated, repeats. We've created hard won documents embracing the Magna Carta and common law—centered around care, which has been with us much longer than code.

Care is also older than law. It is instinct: to protect, to notice, to respond. In the world of humans and animals, it's what keeps us alive, especially the vulnerable. In human made processes and institutions, it's what justice is supposed to be. But in the artificial algorithmic systems and models we are building now, it has been an after thought. Or left out entirely.

The phrase *duty of care* has ethical and legal meaning, but the idea behind it is plain. It means that power—whether it's a state, a system, or a line of code—has an obligation not to harm—to act, or not act, with the well-being of others in mind. The Magna Carta wasn't the beginning of this idea, but it was one of its turning points: a moment when people said that even kings could be bound by care, by restraint, by law.

Today, our kings are digital—built by companies, optimized for profit, immune to borders. They govern invisibly, through patterns and metrics. They decide who is seen and who is skipped, who is flagged, who is forgotten. And yet, in the U.S., they answer to no one—at least not yet.

Part I of this book shines a light on real systems—like Horizon IT and Robodebt—to expose a striking absence of care in the algorithms we increasingly rely on. It reveals what happens when the code that now so deeply touches our lives evolves faster than law: once algorithms are installed, they can become essential. Once we have invested so much in them, they become dug into society like cement. As a result, user and expert complaints sometimes fall on deaf ears. Because of the imperfect social context in which they operate, this situation becomes a perfect storm—an algorithmic disaster that wrongly upends lives and takes years and sometimes decades to make right. Part I also reveals some of the algorithms (and people) that have already made it to the civil and criminal courts.

Part II explores how people (governments, lawyers, corporations, etc.) are beginning to respond. Important laws have already passed in many countries and many more are in progress. It shows these laws are being developed unevenly in scope and scale. Some countries treat algorithms as tools. Others as threats. More than a few (the majority) treat them as responsibilities. In these scattered efforts—some bold, some bureaucratic—we can see a new kind of legal terrain taking shape. It is a hopeful legal terrain because it is being shaped around care and protection for people.

The goal of this book is to help us realize that in this special moment, we are not only users of these systems, we live along side them. And that means we need to have a stake in how they're built. We are the authors and inheritors of law and the authors and designers of code. This means we are also the ones choosing to put care at the heart of the new world we co-inhabit with algorithms. Through the pages of this book you will see the very real human struggles we face in creating this world. It may help us live more easily with automation.

Book Organization

Part I has 6 chapters and introduces the idea of ADOC. It covers both the reactive crisis-driven response we are having to our present situation and also the deeper, ethical stance we need to have—the one representing our values as they relate to the Magna Carta and common law. Part II contains 9 chapters, each covering a different country's policies, regulations and frameworks. What you find is that while countries have some shared concepts, there are unique differences. Where crises and public scandals have already occurred (e.g., Australia, Nederlands) countries are moving quickly to prevent harm, while others are taking baby steps. Some places are addressing narrow areas of technology application while others are focusing on a broader approach. New York, for example, is developing an AI Bill of Rights, and the Nederlands is developing a society wide education program. Each chapter covers key elements of works in progress as well as completed frameworks.

The Appendix has some surprises: it covers the countries that are using AI to actually build laws and "govern-by-AI." There is also a Glossary to help alleviate the need to look up new terms or acronyms.

Some of you may already know, at present, there aren't many federal AI laws in the U.S., with little incentive to change that. Further, many systems of oversight have been recently dismantled. This may seem backwards and dash hope, but remember that while individual accountability mechanisms acting alone are usually weak, success can still happen through the application of many different systems acting together. In researching for this book, this is what we have found. It seems the whole world is waking up to the need to care. In our opinion, this makes it all the more critical to bake duty of care directly into our designs and code. We believe there are many people out there who care and practice duty of care. This book is for them. Pass it on.

TERMS: algorithm; Algorithmic Duty of Care; ADOC; Oblivatronix; algorithmication; *platformification; prevention; Magna Carta; Horizon IT; Dutch childcare scandal.*

CHAPTER 1 REFERENCES

1. Business World Africa. 2025. Meta Faces $2.4B Lawsuit Over Facebook's Role in Ethiopia. https://bwafrica.com/2025/04/04/meta-faces-2-4b-lawsuit-over-facebooks-role-in-ethiopia/
2. Elliot, V. and Cameron, D. 2022. A New Lawsuit Accuses Meta of Inflaming Civil War in Ethiopia. *Wired.* https://www.wired.com/story/meta-hate-speech-lawsuit-ethiopia/
3. Mason, C. 2025. Artificial Compassion Technology Design. Forthcoming.

CHAPTER 2

ALGORITHMS AND THE MAGNA CARTA

The issue of *duty of care* is as old as power itself: what happens when the very people in positions of authority, or the systems they build, turn out to be indifferent to the suffering they cause, or—worse—act as predators? It's a question that arises in the murky spaces where greed meets power, where indifference festers, and where our institutions, meant to protect, often turn a blind eye. It predates the Magna Carta (1) itself, yet today it resonates in a world governed not by monarchs and lords, but by "digital kings"—CEO's and their unseen algorithms and vast data systems. Their power comes not from a throne but from a boardroom, and lines of code and data that shape economies, elections and lives.

Essentially, the issue of duty of care is this: when the people in power and institutions around us turn out to be predators, or are indifferent to the suffering they cause, what do we do? It's a problem that surfaces in situations where there is a power imbalance or an irresistible temptation (necessity?) for profit. Fortunately, most societies uphold systems of conscience and justice where grievances can be aired. In legal, ethical and cultural circles this consciousness of care is described as *duty of care*. It impacts healthcare, business, and professional services. The concept of duty in caring is fundamental in every country whose laws and constitutions are touched by the Magna Carta, which established principles closely related to the ideas of a duty of care.

While it wasn't explicitly framed in those terms, the Magna Carta introduced the idea that those in power have an obligation to act responsibly and prevent harm to those under their rule. Specifically a key component of duty of care ensures that: *those who hold power, whether over land, wealth, or people, are accountable for their actions and must exercise reasonable care to avoid causing harm.*

In the 13th century, England's Magna Carta laid the groundwork for what we now call duty of care—a principle that emerged from the simple, almost naïve, belief that no person, not even a king, was above the law (1). This document directly and indirectly influenced legal systems, constitutions and bills of rights in newly formed countries ranging from the United States to Canada and Australia, and after World War II, to Japan, Sweden and Germany. It also contributed to the United Nations Universal Declaration of Human Rights. Though not directly incorporated into French law, it inspired thinkers like Jean-Jacques Rousseau and Montesquieu, who warned of the dangers of despotism, a form of government where absolute power is concentrated in the hands of one person. He argued that such a system leads to corruption and injustice, as there are no checks on the ruler's power. Such thinking influenced the unshakable mantle of American founders like Benjamin Franklin and Thomas Jefferson and many others in Europe. In effect, the Magna Carta and its subsequent influence created a widespread culture that valued caring for people, starting at the highest level: those in positions of authority must care for their people—be it through justice, fairness, or the protection of rights.

Algorithms and Empires

Fast forward to today, and the world has changed, but the central issue remains the same. Instead of kings and queens, we now have tech CEOs, algorithms and vast data systems. The analogy is clear: those in charge of algorithms with the power to influence millions of lives are not unlike the kings of old. The decisions of algorithms impact jobs, loans, education, healthcare, and more, wielding influence over the lives of hundreds of millions of users. Some social media platforms alone, such as X (formerly Twitter) and Facebook (now Meta), have user bases larger than entire nations.

With 3.07 billion monthly active users, Meta's reach far exceeds the populations of both Brazil (around 215 million) and Indonesia (around 275 million) (2). In fact, Facebook's user base is larger than that of any single nation except China and India. X, with 500 million users, surpasses the population of the United States (approximately 330 million) and exceeds the size of countries like Brazil or Indonesia (3).

Algorithms may not sit on thrones, but the people controlling them hold immense power. As you will see in the pages ahead, even smaller algorithms—while not nearly as massive as these platforms—can profoundly shape people's lives. And, just like a monarch's power, must be tempered by a duty of care. This analogy illustrates why the Magna Carta remains relevant today and why Algorithmic Duty of Care is essential.

You might think of this as an abstraction—an intellectual debate with little relevance to daily life. But consider where decisions are made now. The algorithms governing these platforms and systems are the "kings" of today's world, and their power—over lives, decisions, and outcomes—is both far-reaching and, in many cases, unchecked. In the realm of social media, Generative AI, government services and and even accounting systems, duty of care is largely absent. Further, there are currently no protections against those in power over such Algorithm and Data Systems.

In modern legal frameworks, "duty of care" governs how those in authority—governments, corporations, and institutions—must act to protect individuals from harm. Comparing the restrictions placed on King John in the Magna Carta to a modern duty of care framework is a fair analogy: both are about ensuring that those who wield power are held accountable and that their decisions do not unnecessarily harm others. The algorithms shaping our lives—and the corporations controlling them—are now central to decision-making in society. The concept of ADOC is rooted in this same principle: algorithms and data systems must have a stake in human welfare.

A shift has occurred. Monarchs once held dominion over land, their power confined to borders. Today, algorithms move without restriction, crossing continents, binding systems, deciding outcomes. Their architects, the 'digital kings,' rarely seen, govern in data. They shape economies, politics, and personal lives, aligning themselves, at times, with those who still wear crowns. The Magna Carta, once a demand for accountability in governance, now finds relevance in the weightless, borderless world of algorithms and data systems.

While the Magna Carta is a document of global consequence, it doesn't override today's legislation. However in places where duty of care remains undefined it can still provide guidance. The world we now co-inhabit with algorithms is such a place.

The argument presented here is that we need both a legal and technical framework. The present approach, which is to rely solely on human oversight and the development of laws (as well as policies and regulations) has simply not been successful. Unlike the algorithmic systems under human oversight that failed, in cases like Robodebt (4) and Horizon IT (5), systems intentionally designed with duty of care "baked in" have the potential to protect people in ways that our present approach alone cannot.

First, legislative processes can be slow and hindered by political interests, disagreements and competing priorities. Further, they often fail to keep up with the pace of technological change. This is problematic because although we presently have no legal framework for Algorithmic or Data Duty of Care, lives are already being impacted. By contrast, algorithmic and data solutions designed to include duty of care can be preventive. While legal frameworks only address issues after harm has already occurred, algorithmic systems designed with duty of care can proactively ensure people's safety and rights are considered and respected as part of decision making and problem solving.

Second, algorithms can be tailored to comply with local regulations and, if necessary, global concerns, such as climate change, data privacy, and financial transparency. Also, when issues transcend national borders, algorithms can be used to more quickly implement universal standards and regulations. By contrast, legislative bodies may take years (if not decades) to enact such changes. In the upcoming sections you will see there are many more reasons why it will be helpful to us to bake the idea of duty of care into our designs, codes and algorithms. For example, in the U.S., regulations—especially those concerning AI—are sparse and may not be established for some time. In fact some of the guidelines and federal regulations are being rolled back.

You might say that when it comes to public safety and corporate algorithms, we are walking a path we have never walked before. In the pages ahead, we look closely at these issues. What you will learn quite naturally makes the case for the theme of this book: we need to infuse human compassion and caring into technology design itself.

We believe the idea of Algorithmic Duty of Care, or ADOC, will be the basis for much discussion that is yet to come, and may even become the foundation of legal frameworks of our technological future. We are building a world where we co-exist and co-evolve with technology. A duty of care for this part of our lives is currently missing. We need this discussion urgently.

Duty of Care

Through a series of scandals and crises, we are discovering that the people in charge of such systems are increasingly failing to protect us, not just ethically but also socially.

When something goes wrong with automatic decisions, algorithms or other software, despite a large number of concerns and complaints, despite investigative reports by experts, algorithmic concerns have often been ignored by people in charge who should have cared. And in some cases, where there have been governmental or judicial investigations, leaders have lied during such investigations, leaving people embarrassed and ashamed in front of friends, family and community. Importantly, it leaves them without justice for life altering abuses that went on for years and sometimes decades. In places such as the U.S., federal laws governing duty of care in AI have been removed and the idea of ADOC does not yet exist in the minds of corporations or bodies of law. So what choice do we have to uphold the values of our society other than to design duty of care into technology?

Algorithmic harm has already occurred, and without awareness and the establishment of a culture, ethos, and legal precedent for Algorithmic Duty of Care, such harm will continue. Ignoring this reality once we are aware of it is both reckless and negligent. The point of this book is to raise awareness about how duty of care applies to the design and use of algorithms, particularly in contexts where they significantly impact people's lives, safety, and society.

In fact this entire book is really about baking an Algorithmic Duty of Care directly into the design of our tools, systems, video games, and so on. This topic is covered in detail in *Designing Artificial Compassion Technology (6)*. When we design technology this way it reflects the values we have held in societies around the world since the inception of the Magna Carta. The idea of baking duty of care into our designs certainly moves us out of the Oblivatronix Era we live in now, where the systems, devices and algorithms surrounding us are oblivious to the need to take people's welfare into account. In effect, it is one approach to creating Artificial Compassion Technology.

Why We Need Algorithmic Duty of Care

In recent years, we have witnessed the rise of algorithms responsible for human suffering that has lasted years, even though they had human oversight. This was possible not only because of the slow pace of justice, but also the inherent failings of our human nature. Those in power over such algorithms further slowed our ability to acknowledge and stop the suffering by ignoring complaints and by hiding information and lying in investigations and court proceedings. Extreme examples (that we know of so far) include public scandals such as Robodebt in Australia, the Dutch childcare benefits scandal (Toeslagenaffaire) and the Horizon IT postal scandal in the UK. The damage that occurred in these human managed cases raises multiple red flags.

In all three of these cases, the people in power over such algorithms falsely accused victims (users) of wrongdoing—upending families, communities and lives, and in some cases, ending human lives. The suffering went on for years despite expert warnings. Those in power ignored these concerns. In court, leaders who should have protected and cared for the public covered up failures, lost material evidence and shifted blame. In these court cases, the foundational principle of duty of care—intended to protect the public—was utterly non-existent in those in power over these algorithms. The principle of those in power having a duty of care over the public, the idea of a "king" (CEO) being subject to the same laws as citizens, was nowhere to be found. This is a problem in need of a solution.

Algorithms, agents, decision making, and other kinds of systems are increasingly influencing critical decisions that impact our lives: who gets a job, a loan, or even justice. New algorithms may also determine back taxes owed and automatically take money from your bank accounts, or compute a considerably less amount of retirement than you had calculated. Yet when these algorithms go wrong, the consequences are devastating. Human institutions and leaders are routinely failing to address these injustices swiftly—or at all. We need to address this situation before even more tragedy strikes.

Here lies the crux of this book: we need algorithmic and data solutions that anticipate and prevent injustice *before* lives and communities are upended or destroyed. Alone, our existing systems of human oversight are inadequate to protect us from the harm of unchecked algorithms. Worse, they appear to be used in the service of people in power with shortcomings, such as greed and dishonesty, when they should be safeguarding us against them. The answer offered here is to bring the concept of duty of care into the algorithms themselves with Algorithmic Duty of Care and Data Duty Of Care (DDOC). Unlike the duty of care we are familiar with, which rests solely on human accountability, an algorithmic or data approach also embeds responsibility directly into the technologies shaping our world. Naturally, not all algorithms and technologies will need this.

Inspired by the Magna Carta and long-standing legal principles, algorithms and designs that embrace ADOC and DDOC can be proactive in preventing harm and offer tangible benefits. In effect, they serve as the guardrails that our institutions and leaders have failed to provide. Rather than merely addressing the social or human reasons behind ethical failures, ADOC and DDOC embed the duty of care directly into our designs and code.

In the following pages, we dive into the social challenges that algorithms present and explore the centuries-old principles of duty of care. We'll see that if we are to reflect our values in the technologies that are so closely influencing our lives, embedding duty of care into our algorithms, agents, systems, devices and so on, is crucial. Establishing ADOC and DDOC can be part of a framework for future regulations and ethical guidelines that govern the use of algorithms. They can help shape the development of laws and standards that *protect us from harm in an age when our daily interactions are increasingly shaped by systems we can neither fully see nor control.* This is a key issue, for example, in governing by algorithm. We take a closer look at some of these important ideas in the next chapter.

TERMS: Horizon IT; Magna Carta; kings; FaceBook; world population; ADOC; DDOC.

CHAPTER 2 REFERENCES

1. United Kingdom Parliament. 2025. Magna Carta. https://www.parliament.uk/magnacarta/
2. Global Social Media Statistics. 2025. *DataReportal.* https://datareportal.com/social-media-users
3. WorldOMeter. 2025. Countries in the world by population 2025. https://www.worldometers.info/world-population/population-by-country/ Retrieved April 15 2025.
4. The Crown. 2024. Post Office Horizon IT INQUIRY. What's Next for the Inquiry? https://www.postofficehorizoninquiry.org.uk
5. Royal Commission. 2023. Robodebt Royal Commission—Overview of Final Report. https://www.apra.gov.au/sites/default/files/2024-02/Robodebt%20Royal%20Commision%20-%20Overview%20of%20Final%20Report.pdf
6. Mason. 2023. The Emotion Organon. ISBN 979-885-1933-400

CHAPTER 3

ALGORITHMIC AND DATA DUTY OF CARE

No one remembers the first algorithm that decided a human's fate. There wasn't a hearing, or a headline. This is not science fiction. It's our new world.

In this chapter we look closer at Algorithmic Duty of Care (ADOC). We explore some of the challenges that come with the algorithmification movement and include three case studies: Horizon IT, Robodebt and Toeslagenaffaire (the Dutch children's welfare system—kinderopvangtoeslagaffaire). The issues we describe also relate to data systems, hence we will also use the term "Data Duty of Care."

The Robodebt Algorithm

In a government office in Canberra, a man received a debt notice from a machine. He hadn't spoken to anyone. He hadn't filed anything recently. Still, the letter said he owed money. He didn't know the number had come from an algorithm.

One example of the need for Algorithmic Duty of Care is Australia's Robodebt, an automatic debt collection algorithm, which ended in a $1.8 billion dollar class action settlement (1, 2). If you're looking for a corporate bottom line, this might be it. But there is more. According to Services Australia, the branch of the Australian government that oversaw the system, 2,030 people that received a Robodebt-related letter subsequently died, many of whom were vulnerable (mentally ill, disabled or retired); some committed suicide after receiving notices from the Robodebt algorithm. A series of investigations, senate hearings and Royal Commission investigations occurred. It seems very clear that people could use some help with preventing these costly, painful problems. Unfortunately, this case is only one of many.

The Childcare Benefits Algorithm

Our second example is the Dutch childcare benefits scandal (Dutch: kinderopvangtoeslagaffaire or toeslagenaffaire). The controversy emerged from the implementation of a new childcare benefits law in 2005, which led to systemic issues in the Dutch Tax and Customs Administration. Between 2005 and 2019, approximately 26,000 parents were wrongly accused of welfare fraud, resulting in demands to repay substantial amounts of money. This led to severe financial hardship, including bankruptcies, the loss of housing, and even the removal of children from their homes.

Between 2015 and 2021, it is estimated that 1,675 children were removed from their homes due to the wrongful accusations against their parents. This figure which includes children placed in foster care or residential institutions has also been estimated to be much higher (3). The scandal gained public attention in September 2018, prompting investigations that criticized the Tax and Customs Administration's procedures as discriminatory, particularly affecting parents with foreign backgrounds and characterized by institutional biases. A parliamentary inquiry found that "unprecedented injustice" had been done to innocent families and the crisis ultimately resulted in the resignation of Prime Minister Mark Rutte's cabinet in January 2021. Further, the tax authority used overly strict and discriminatory algorithms, which flagged people for minor errors or missing documents. A zero-tolerance fraud policy was applied aggressively, without due process. It was further revealed that the algorithms were programmed with ethnic profiling—a majority of the accused were people with dual nationality or a migration background, raising serious issues about systemic bias.

Efforts to reunite families have been underway, with targeted support programs offering assistance such as legal aid and housing support. As of 2023, over 500 parents had reached out to the Support Team for help in reuniting with their children. At present, many children have been reunited with their families. However, some remain in care, and the reunification process continues for others (4).

This case example is a terrible tragedy. It shows how human bias can be embedded in an algorithm. It also shows us another example of how long it can take to resolve such algorithmic situations. The uncovering of the *Toeslagenaffaire* was a slow-burning process that took years to come fully into the light.

Many affected parents began filing complaints and appealing the harsh decisions from the Dutch Tax Authority. But for years, these were mostly dismissed or handled case by case, without seeing the full systemic pattern. Some of these families organized and became more vocal—sharing their stories with members of parliament and journalists. The real turning point came in 2018, when Dutch news outlet Trouw, in collaboration with RTL Nieuws, started publishing deep investigative reports.

The algorithm, a rule-based system, was developed and operated by the Dutch Tax and Customs Administration in collaboration with the Ministry of Social Affairs and Employment. The algorithm incorporated nationality as a risk factor, disproportionately flagging non-Dutch nationals, especially those with dual nationality, for fraud. This allowed the system to make biased decisions (5). It is reported that the system operated as a "black box," meaning applicants and even civil servants lacked insight into how decisions were made, hindering accountability and recourse. On the surface, this seems fishy, because usually rule based systems can explain their chain of reasoning.

To their credit, the Dutch are working diligently to prevent the situation from happening again: they have embraced the EU AI Act and are active in educating all ages of the public on AI from primary school to senior citizens. For more on what the Dutch are doing to prevent these situations see Chapter 13.

The Horizon IT Algorithm

Our third and last example, the British Postal Scandal, also known as the Horizon IT scandal, shows there is a need for both Algorithm and Data Duty of Care. It began in 1999 and, as of 2025, has finally become a criminal investigation. As mentioned previously, the criminal trial is not expected to begin before 2027! (6). According to evidence gathered by investigations, it seems more than a coincidence that the people in charge ignored the suffering of those afflicted. In fact, it appears to have been intentional, directed and a very sophisticated manipulation. Former U.K. Prime Minister Rishi Sunak described the subpostmaster convictions as “one of the greatest miscarriages of justice in our nation’s history” (7). However, it took a movie (“Mr. Bates vs. the Post Office”) to make this case part of the public consciousness.

Following the show’s broadcast in January 2024, there was a surge in public outrage, prompting renewed calls for compensation and accountability. The series helped humanize the victims, making their struggles more tangible to the general public. As a result, the UK government intensified efforts to resolve the scandal, including discussions on financial redress and further investigations into those responsible

The British Postal Scandal involved accounting software used in the post offices of England, Wales and Northern Ireland. It “involved the Post

Office pursuing thousands of innocent subpostmasters for apparent financial shortfalls caused by faults in Horizon, an accounting software system developed by Fujitsu. Between 1999 and 2015, more than 900 subpostmasters were wrongly convicted of theft, fraud and false accounting based on faulty Horizon data, with about 700 prosecutions carried out by the Post Office. Other subpostmasters who were prosecuted but not convicted, were forced to cover faulty shortfalls with their own money, or had their contracts terminated. The court cases, criminal convictions, imprisonments, loss of livelihoods and homes, debts, and bankruptcies led to stress, illness, family breakdowns and at least four suicides" (8).

Human Guardrails

As illustrated by these three examples, human oversight may at first appear to be a solid strategy, but in reality, it has proven tragically unstable. Although harm must first be *noticed* before it's even acknowledged, even those who notice may not act. Further, even when it is noticed, efforts to address algorithmic and data harm often occur long *after* the damage is initially reported. Moreover, restitution for the victims can take a long time. During this wait victims continue to suffer harm: they go to prison, become addicts, lose their families and reputation in the community, and sometimes commit suicide. In one case, a pregnant woman went to prison and gave birth while in jail (9).

"Notice-and-takedown" policies are frequently used by social media platforms, for example. A "notice-and-takedown" approach places the burden on users or customers who have experienced harm to notice-and-report it, which can add insult to injury. Importantly, during the time it takes to react to notice-and-reports, harm continues to occur.

These examples also show that the way we currently approach these problems, with human guardrails, is not working. What if, instead of leaving it up to users to notice and report harm, or waiting until after it has occurred, we bake "duty of care" into our algorithms, agents, classifiers, games, and other systems. In this way, even if the people involved are corrupt, the system provides guardrails against unethical decisions and behaviors. What would be nice is to have is a black box for CEOs and everything that goes on in a company, including its information, sort of like the black boxes used in an aircraft cockpit. Practically speaking though, how do we do this?

Fire in the Brake Lines

From what we've seen so far, individual approaches alone are weak. Human oversight, when it works, can enable us to respond quickly when harm is detected. But reliance on human oversight has proven untrustworthy. Robodebt and Horizon IT systems had oversight, yet failed spectacularly. While essential to an overall approach, human oversight remains vulnerable to human failings—bias, greed, and ethical lapses. Advances in diagnostic cognitive neuroscience mean it is possible to, in theory, scan people's brains to determine their ethical fitness. However, this approach is prohibitively expensive, so would not scale well. It may also be objectionable to most people.

Legal systems, though crucial, are also limited. They are a reactive solution, addressing harm after it has occurred rather than preventing it. Laws, no matter how well-crafted, cannot prevent deception in court or stop harm in its tracks. Also, because litigation moves at a slow pace, it allows damage to continue unchecked. It's a bit like watching a train wreck unfold in slow motion.

This is where Algorithmic Duty of Care, or ADOC, offers a breakthrough. By embedding safeguards within technology itself, ADOC allows us to design for prevention rather than just punishment. Unlike legislation, which struggles to keep pace with technological change, algorithms can be adapted quickly to reflect emerging standards. They can also be tailored to local regulations while also addressing global concerns like climate change, data privacy, and financial transparency, areas where legal frameworks often lag for years.

Importantly, ADOC is not a silver bullet—it must work in concert with laws, human oversight and other methods, such as embedding a duty of care into designs, data and algorithms. No approach is perfect, but by bringing many approaches together, we have a greater chance of avoiding and preventing disasters.

There are other reasons why it will be helpful to us to bake the idea of duty of care into our designs, data and algorithms. For example, in the U.S., federal regulations—especially the ones concerning AI—are sparse and may not be established for some time. In fact the main (only) U.S. federal AI protection was rolled back in January 2025 (10).

You might say that when it comes to public safety and algorithms, we are navigating uncharted waters. In the pages ahead, we look closer at the intersection of duty of care and the Magna Carta and corporate algorithms. What you will learn quite naturally makes the case for the theme of this book: we need to infuse human compassion and caring into technology design itself.

We believe the idea of Algorithmic Duty of Care will be the basis for much discussion that is yet to come, and may even become the foundation of legal frameworks of our technological future. We are building a world where we co-exist and co-evolve with technology. A duty of care for this part of our lives is currently missing. We need it urgently.

The Rise of Algorithmic Compassion

One way duty of care could be expressed programmatically in the Robodebt algorithm is a hardship clause or constraint. A hardship clause would allow the algorithm to have guardrails against harming people.

Namely, it can make exceptions (and explain these exceptions) in its decision making, if such decisions would result in interfering with life-sustaining medicines, shelter, health or safety.

One way to implement such hardship guardrails would be the use of RAG, or Retrieval Augmented Generation. RAG is a focused collection of knowledge that can act as a second stage filter for answers or decisions created by a Generative AI system. The RAG system can compare trusted information regarding social or human welfare to the AI system's response, ensuring the decisions or answers provided by the system stay aligned with social values and best practices. Other approaches include rule-based systems, content filtering, required explanation and justification, and so on. There are also approaches including people, such as human-in-the-loop, and layered approaches involving technical, procedural and human oversight.

However, approaches involving human oversight, even those with third party oversight, have failings. An example of this is the Australian National Anti-Corruption Commission (NACC), which itself became the subject of an investigation during the resolution of the Robodebt Scheme by the Royal Commission (11, 12). In other words, the party assigned to investigate the scandal was itself investigated. Such is the fate of the human race. The position of this book is that it is necessary to develop multiple approaches including legal and algorithmic solutions.

Approaches to address harm that involve just people are fraught with challenges, but we can leverage our technology designs to address this. Both Algorithmic and Data Duty of Care can help prevent the years of algorithmic harm and injustice that people currently face. This is Algorithmic Compassion rising. It is what Asimov's First Law Corollary is all about. Here is the First Law Corollary:

Asimov's First Law Corollary

A device, algorithm or computing system may not injure a human being or, through inaction, allow a human being to come to harm. Further, whenever possible and useful, a device, algorithm or computing system shall be helpful and support a human being with positivity, optimism and care.

The corollary empowers programmers, designers, and those in positions of power within institutions to do more than simply react after what can sometimes, be decades of on-going damage. This is important because presently, it can take years (decades) of complaints and reports before anything is done or changed. The Algorithmic Duty of Care approach is proactive. When we embrace it, we recognize that algorithms can, in fact, prevent or minimize human suffering. When we begin designing with this in mind, we not only improve our present circumstances but shape a better future. While algorithms may not know us or care for us like another person would, they can, at the very least, take into account our vulnerabilities and make decisions that support us. This idea is part of the EU AI Act (13, 14). This is what we can expect from systems, games, devices, and more in the Post-Oblivatronix era, an era in which we design algorithms to care about whether we live or die. Algorithmic and Data Duty of Care are examples of Artificial Compassion Technology. The extent to which we do this is up to us.

Terms: *Algorithmic Compassion; Horizon IT; Toeslagenaffaire; Dutch child welfare; Robodebt; ADOC; DDOC; Duty of Care; Asimov's First Law Corollary; proactive; reactive; Algorithmic Compassion.*

CHAPTER 3 REFERENCES

1. Henriques-Gomes, L. 2021. Robodebt: court approves $1.8bn settlement for victims of government's 'shameful' failure. *The Guardian.* https://www.theguardian.com/australia-news/2021/jun/11/robodebt-court-approves-18bn-settlement-for-victims-of-governments-shameful-failure
2. Gorden Legal. 2021. Robodebt class action. https://gordonlegal.com.au/robodebt-class-action

3. Vision Times. 2022. 2,090 Dutch Children Taken by State in Tax Agency Benefits Scandal. https://www.visiontimes.com/2022/12/08/dutch-children-seized-tax-agency-benefits-scandal.html
4. Government.NL. 2023. Targeted support offered to victims of the childcare benefits scandal with children taken into care. https://www.government.nl/topics/youth-policy/news/2023/09/18/targeted-support-offered-to-victims-of-the-childcare-benefits-scandal-with-children-taken-into-care
5. O'Neil, C. 2017. *Weapons of Math Destruction.* Crown Publishers. NY.
6. Criminal Cases Review Commission. 2024. The CCRC and Post Office/ Horizon cases. https://ccrc.gov.uk/news/the-ccrc-and-post-office-horizon-cases/
7. GOV.UK. 2024. Government to quash wrongful Post Office convictions. https://www.gov.uk/government/news/government-to-quash-wrongful-post-office-convictions
8. "British Post Office scandal" Wikipedia. https://en.wikipedia.org/wiki/British_Post_Office_scandal
9. Croft, J. 2024. Post office operator wrongly jailed while pregnant rejects executive's apology. *The Guardian.* https://www.theguardian.com/uk-news/2024/apr/11/former-post-office-md-sorry-for-celebrating-pregnant-operators-conviction
10. White House. 2025. Fact Sheet: President Donald J. Trump Takes Action to Enhance America's AI Leadership. *White House Executive Order by Donald Trump.* https://www.whitehouse.gov/fact-sheets/2025/01/fact-sheet-president-donald-j-trump-takes-action-to-enhance-americas-ai-leadership/
11. The Royal Commission. 2023. Report of the Royal Commission into the Robodebt Scheme. https://robodebt.royalcommission.gov.au/system/files/2023-09/rrc-accessible-full-report.PDF
12. National Anti-Corruption Commission. 2025. Parliament of Australia. https://www.nacc.gov.au/
13. European Union. 2025. The EU Artificial Intelligence Act. https://artificialintelligenceact.eu/high-level-summary/
14. European Union. 2016. REGULATION (EU) 2016/679 OF THE EUROPEAN PARLIAMENT AND OF THE COUNCIL. Official Journal of the European Union. https://eur-lex.europa.eu/eli/reg/2016/679/oj

CHAPTER 4

ALGORITHMS AND SOCIAL POWER

The Robodebt, Toeslagenaffaire and Horizon IT scandals are three of the more visible (and recent) reasons why we need an Algorithmic (and Data) Duty of Care. These systems also visibly demonstrate how algorithms and systems exist within social power structures.

In all three cases, Robodebt, Toeslagenaffaire and Horizon IT, people endured suffering for years while leaders in those power structures ignored problem reports from victims, system users and even experts. For Horizon IT, these situations dragged on for additional years due to repeated, lengthy investigations that were conducted, including Royal Commissions, which only concluded at the end of 2024. That is an astonishing quarter of a century!

During this time, many of those falsely accused in the Horizon IT case saw their lives unravel. Some turned to drugs and alcohol, others lost their reputations, homes, communities and families. Some committed suicide. The British Post Office not only pursued criminal convictions against the subpostmasters, but once convicted, they also secured court orders to seize their assets. Only now, after the subpostmasters have been exonerated, are the police beginning to investigate possible criminal behavior. By February 2024, 4000 subpostmasters were slated to receive compensation for the wrongful accusations and prosecutions they endured. The government has budgeted 1 billion pounds for compensation (or approximately 1.3 billion U.S. dollars). See: https://en.wikipedia.org/wiki/British_Post_Office_scandal

Had Artificial Compassion systems been in place, had an Algorithmic Duty of Care been part of early design thinking, the tragic upending of lives, homes, families, health, and money could have been prevented.

Aligning Technology With Our Values

Caring for and protecting one another is a value shared by human beings and even animals every where in the world. Bus drivers care for their passengers; physicians care for their patients; teachers care for their students; parents care for their children, and so on. It is the fabric of our society, culture, religion and family. Yet, in the technologies we are building and surrounding ourselves with, there remains a significant blind spot to these deeply held values. Systems that impact our lives, whether in small or large ways, have been designed to solve a problem (or puzzle) or automate a process, generally without consideration for the care required to prevent negative human or social consequences.

The reasons for this situation are a complex interplay of human psychology and behavior, including tech culture, Asperger's syndrome (which impacts emotional and social awareness), organizational psychopathy, lack of social or cultural common sense, confirmation bias, over-trust in technology, ignorance, etc. People are solely responsible for the application and oversight of such algorithms and systems. Unfortunately, this strategy isn't working. For example, consider the teacher evaluation system, EVAAS, created by the company SAS (1). Public schools used EVAAS to evaluate teachers for contract renewal but it incorrectly recommended terminating contracts with some of their best teachers, e.g., Daniel Santos (2).

Another unfortunate example involves the TikTok Kia Challenge ("Kia Challenge" 2025). Social media postings showed how easy it was to steal or carjack Kia and Hyundai cars, causing the number of thefts of these brands to skyrocket around the world. According to the National Insurance Crime Bureau, "Hyundai and Kia vehicle thefts surged nationwide in the summer of 2022, increasing 95% from 2021" (3). Children as young as 11 years old have been involved in car vandalizing, theft, and police chases, resulting in injuries, fatal mortalities and jail time (4). These incidents are snatching away young lives and ruining futures. This social media phenomenon may be linked to Grand Theft Auto, one of the world's most popular and best-selling video games. Players score points by stealing cars/carjacking, killing people and evading the police. Top players compete to kill the most and post their scores in public.

These examples, along with Horizon IT, Toeslagenaffaire and Robodebt, are not exhaustive; there are others, such as live face recognition systems which have proven to be inaccurate when used by law enforcement (5). In effect, the prevalence of such systems in use today means that unless we change the way we design such systems, in other words, so that they intentionally "protect us and do no harm," people will continue to be injured by them.

The solution proposed here is to infuse the algorithms, systems and devices themselves with the knowledge, data, and decision making that will do no harm and protect and care about us. It's a duty of care expressed through technology.

In essence, an algorithmic response to harm involves the creation of designs, code, and software requirements that address underlying issues such as neglect, lack of care, and insufficient preventative measures. These efforts aim, at least in part, to mitigate the problems stemming from human shortcomings. Designing in this way is a natural act of compassion. This approach heralds a new era of devices, algorithms, video games, virtual reality, and more—tools that prioritize user well-being not through regulations alone but also via thoughtful and considerate design.

Achieving this requires embracing an Algorithmic (Data) Duty of Care. But what exactly does adopting an Algorithmic Duty of Care mean?

Is it necessary for an Algorithmic Duty of Care to be defined by law? In the next sections we review some of the foundational ideas that relate to the commonly held concept of duty of care, including its relationship to law and government, and explore the general concept of duty of care as it relates to the Magna Carta and corporate algorithms.

General Duty of Care

The concept of duty of care is embedded in legal frameworks around the world, from the U.S. and U.K. to commonwealth nations and beyond. As mentioned previously, it refers to the obligation of individuals or organizations to act with reasonable care in ways that avoid foreseeably causing harm to others, i.e., to act responsibly. This principle is foundational in fields like law, healthcare, insurance, business, and education. If someone breaches this duty and causes harm, they can be held responsible for damages or injuries that occur.

Duty of care can take many forms across different contexts, but its essence is always about acting responsibly to prevent harm to others. Here are some notable examples:

1. **Healthcare:** Doctors and nurses have a duty of care to provide safe and effective medical treatment to their patients. For instance, following proper protocols during surgeries or administering the correct medication dosage.

2. **Education:** Teachers have a duty of care to ensure the safety and well-being of their students. This can include supervising activities, addressing bullying, or providing a safe learning environment.

3. **Workplace:** Employers owe a duty of care to their employees to ensure they have a safe work environment. For example, providing proper

equipment, training, and implementing safety measures to avoid workplace accidents.

4. **Product Safety:** Companies have a duty of care to their customers to ensure that their products are safe to use. For instance, a food manufacturer must follow hygiene standards to prevent contamination.
5. **Legal:** Attorneys owe a duty of care to their clients to provide competent legal representation, safeguarding confidentiality, and acting in their best interests.
6. **Public Spaces:** Local authorities or property owners are responsible for maintaining public spaces like sidewalks and parks to prevent hazards, such as fixing broken pavement or removing ice.
7. **Transportation:** Pilots, drivers, and transportation operators have a duty of care to ensure passenger safety. For example, airline pilots must conduct pre-flight safety checks, and bus drivers should adhere to traffic rules.

These examples demonstrate how duty of care is a vital principle in many aspects of life, fostering trust and accountability in our social interactions and systems. What's missing from the above list is a section on the standard duty of care for technology and algorithms. The reason it's absent is that such norms do not yet exist—at least not in the United States. This is a significant problem. It's also the reason for this chapter.

While we introduce the concepts of Algorithmic and Data Duty of Care, we need to expand this idea more broadly in tech culture and society so that it encompasses all of our technology and algorithms. Software developers and tech companies now have a growing responsibility to ensure their algorithms and systems don't cause harm. A good starting point would be to ensure transparency in AI systems that influence critical decisions, such as those related to our employment, loans, or other significant life outcomes. In fact some individual states, such as Colorado,

California, Illinois and New York are making progress in these areas (6, 7, 8, 9). Progress in this area across the states will hopefully continue to expand in the coming years.

The Magna Carta and The Duty Of Care

Although we have explored the connection between the Magna Carta and the Duty of Care earlier (in Chapter 2), in this section we take a closer look—keeping in mind how they might apply to algorithms and data systems.

As mentioned previously, duty of care is not a modern concept; it has deep historical roots connected to the Magna Carta (and common law). For instance, the Magna Carta established the principle that even the king was subject to the law, not above it. It also laid the groundwork for the right to a fair trial, due process, and protection from arbitrary arrest. These are all relevant to the current moment in technology. This document inspired freedom movements and constitutional reforms worldwide, forming the foundation of much of the modern world as we know it today (10). One example of this is the United Nations' Universal Declaration of Human Rights (11).

Accountability The Magna Carta was a bold declaration that even the king was bound by the law. It took a powerful step in making sure that rulers couldn't act with impunity. They had to answer for their actions. Similarly, "duty of care" insists that individuals and organizations are accountable for their actions, especially when those actions can harm others. It's about holding people to a standard of responsibility that ensures their actions won't cause harm.

Protection of Rights The Magna Carta's main mission was to protect rights—most notably, freedom from unlawful imprisonment and the guarantee of a fair trial. Its message: individuals should not be treated unjustly. "Duty of care" plays a similar role, though more broadly. It safeguards people from harm, requiring others to act with consideration and responsibility. It's a principle found throughout many legal and professional fields, and protects people from neglect or injury.

Laying Down Principles The Magna Carta was one of the first documents to lay out clear principles about how people, especially those in power, should behave. These principles laid the groundwork for future laws. The concept of "duty of care", too, is about setting out clear standards—whether in healthcare, business, or public service—that define how people should act responsibly to avoid harm to others.

A Legacy of Legal Influence The Magna Carta didn't just reshape its own era; its influence has resonated throughout history, shaping modern concepts of law and rights. It shaped documents like the English Bill of Rights and in the U.S., the Magna Carta's principles of due process, freedom from arbitrary imprisonment, and the rule of law are reflected in the U.S. Constitution and the Bill of Rights. Similarly, "duty of care" has become a cornerstone in modern law, found in everything from tort law to corporate ethics. It is a legal legacy that compels individuals, organizations, and corporations (along with their products) to act responsibly in their impact on others or face accountability.

Summary The Magna Carta and the "duty of care" might seem worlds apart, but both are about the same core idea: making sure people are held accountable for their actions, that they protect the rights of others and that they follow a responsible code of conduct. Whether in medieval England or modern times, these concepts lay the foundation for justice and fairness. Importantly, they ensure that those in positions of power—whether employers, public officials, or others—act in the best interests of those they oversee. You can imagine how these ideas can be helpful in crafting the duty of care for Algorithms and Data Systems.

Though rooted in law, duty of care extends beyond legal frameworks. It is woven into the social fabric of our cultures through ethics, religion, family, and everyday relationships. But in the last twenty years or so, we have created a new social world that is based on technology. So far, that social technical world is largely lawless. In essence, duty of care represents an implicit social contract and although such social contracts are rooted in the physical world, they should also extend to the social technical worlds we are creating. Further, there should also be a mutual responsibility that individuals or entities in those social technical worlds hold towards one another within a community or society that exists within or across such social technical spaces. This is especially important as our physical world and social technical spaces begin to spill over on each other. In the old world, we might say, when this duty is breached, someone has to pay. But by designing algorithmic and data duty of care we engage with prevention.

Corporate Duty of Care in the U.S.

In the U.S. when applied to business and corporate law, the scope of duty of care is notably different from what we have just learned. Executives and board members in U.S. corporations must act not in the best interests of the public, but of shareholders and stakeholders.

This narrow interpretation of corporate duty of care is outdated and problematic in an era where algorithms that are created and controlled by corporations have vast influence over the public. The influence of such algorithms are so significant there is a new word for it — algorithmification. As mentioned earlier, algorithmification refers to the growing use of algorithms to digitize, influence, and control various aspects of life—from employment and college admissions to justice systems, healthcare, news, and advertising of all kinds.

Consider, for instance, the rise of social media platforms over the past decade. These algorithms now shape the lives of millions—if not billions—of people, for better or worse. Take Facebook's controversial Emotional Contagion experiment, which altered the News Feeds of nearly 700,000 users to test their emotional response to positive or negative content. Without users' consent, the study revealed that exposure to negative content led to more negative posts, demonstrating Facebook's power to influence emotions without the users' awareness (12, 13). Critics raised alarms about the potential for large-scale psychological manipulation, an issue that underscores how dramatically the landscape has shifted (14).

The Facebook experiment is evidence that corporate algorithms, which were not a consideration when many of these legal structures were formed, now have the capacity to affect individuals on a massive scale. The current model of corporate duty of care towards the public is outdated in a world where so many people's lives are so profoundly impacted by the algorithms corporations control. If we want to co-exist and co-evolve with algorithms in a way that supports and protects people , we need to align corporate business models with the concept of a duty of care. This is already embraced in much of the world through legal and ethical traditions like those found in the Magna Carta. However, since a legal framework like this is unlikely to happen soon (in the U.S.), the next best thing is to simply design for it.

Design is Faster Than Legislation

In light of the cases we have seen earlier, e.g., Grand Theft Auto, TikTok KIA Challenge, Robodebt, the childhood benefits scandal (Toeslagenaffaire) and the Horizon IT Post Office scandal, etc., it certainly appears that current regulations and laws around algorithms are not tightly aligned with the ideas of the Magna Carta. There is a gap in the legislation (in the U.S.) to ensure individuals and organizations act responsibly to avoid causing harm to others through algorithms, decision making systems, games, and so on. To remedy this, many countries, states and other jurisdictions are creating various kinds of AI Acts. But the issues we raise here mean that the problems we are facing are not strictly limited to AI. An AI Duty of Care is all good and well. And it's a start. But it doesn't cover algorithms in general. The trouble with laws focused on AI is that a company or government or administration can simply say, "well, that's not AI." And this would be true if you're talking about Horizon IT or Robodebt. Places like New York have the right idea by introducing a Bill of Rights to cover "any system making decisions without human intervention" (9). While this covers decision making it does not cover other forms of algorithms that impact our lives such as video games (gamification) and social media platforms (platformification).

Despite this legal gap (around algorithms) in corporate and business law, duty of care remains a foundation of society, woven through culture and religion alike. We live in an era of rapid technological innovation, where the products we create reach into our minds and lives at a scale never seen before. This is what we mean when we say that algorithms are helping to shape our social fabric. This gap is widening. And as the British say, we must "mind the gap". But here's the thing: *we don't have to wait for legislation.* As designers, programmers, and engineers, we can act now. Regulations will come to the U.S. —eventually. In the meantime, we can embed care into our systems by design. The approach in this book proposes just that: a technical foundation built not only on code, but on a duty of care that is based on on advances in human science, medical research, and the long arc of history (15). In the next chapter, we introduce definitions for ADOC and relate it to the Magna Carta.

TERMS: TikTok Challenge; Algorithmification; Platformification; Gamification; Magna Carta.

CHAPTER 4 REFERENCES

1. SAS. 2025. SAS EVAAS for K-12. https://www.sas.com/en_us/software/evaas.html
2. State of Texas Harris County. 2017. Settlement and Full and Final Release Agreement. https://www.aft.org/sites/default/files/media/2017/settlementagreement_houston_100717.pdf
3. Shapiro, K. 2024. Challenging A Viral Vehicle Theft Dare. National Insurance Crime Bureau. https://www.nicb.org/challenging-viral-vehicle-theft-dare
4. Medina, H. 2024. 11-year-old 'KIA BOY' arrested after stealing several cars and sh*oting at people. Albuquerque Police Department Police Chief. https://www.instagram.com/cars/p/C8DFrmjsPZF
5. Morioka, S. 2025. Flawed Facial Recognition Technology Leads to Wrongful Arrest and Historic Settlement. *Michigan Law.* https://quadrangle.michigan.law.umich.edu/issues/winter-2024-2025/flawed-facial-recognition-technology-leads-wrongful-arrest-and-historic
6. California Legislative Information. 2024. *AB-2655 Defending Democracy from Deepfake Deception Act of 2024.* https://leginfo.legislature.ca.gov/faces/billNavClient.xhtml?bill_id=202320240AB2655
7. Legislation of Colorado Government. 2024. SB24-205 Concerning consumer protections in interactions with Artificial Intelligence systems. *General Assembly of the State of Colorado.* https://leg.colorado.gov/sites/default/files/2024a_205_signed.pdf
8. New York State Assembly. 2024. A09430B Oversight of automated decision-making in government act. https://assembly.state.ny.us/leg/?bn=A09430&term=2023&Summary=Y&Actions=Y
9. New York State Senate. 2024. The New York artificial intelligence bill of rights. https://legislation.nysenate.gov/pdf/bills/2023/S8209
10. Goldman, L., Editor. 2018. *Magna Carta: History, Context and Influence.* Institute for Historical Research. University of London Press. London, England. DOI: https://doi.org/10.14296/718.9781909646889
11. United Nations Human Rights. 1948. The Universal Declaration of Human Rights. https://www.un.org/en/about-us/universal-declaration-of-human-rights
12. Kramer, A., Guillory, J. and Hancock, J. 2014. Experimental evidence of massive-scale emotional contagion through social networks. Proc. Natl. Acad. Sci.(PNAS). *111* (24): 8788-8790. https://doi.org/10.1073/pnas.1320040111
13. Kerr, D. 2024. CNET: Senator asks FTC to investigate Facebook's mood study. https://www.warner.senate.gov/public/index.cfm/mobile/issueslegislation?ID=6C730E48-F33F-44E3-B7C9-BCC2A83FDAB0

14. Klitzman, R. And Appelbaum, P. 2014. Facebook's Emotion Experiment: Implications for Research Ethics. The Hastings Center for Bioethics. https://www.thehastingscenter.org/facebooks-emotion-experiment-implications-for-research-ethics/
15. Mason, C. 2023. The Emotion Organon. ISBN 979-885-1933-400

CHAPTER 5

ADOC DEFINED

***Algorithmic Duty of Care (Def):** a moral and legal obligation for any system, algorithm or device—and the institutions responsible for them—to adhere to a standard of reasonable care, avoiding careless acts that could foreseeably harm others, and lead to claims in negligence. An Algorithmic Duty of Care may also include the moral and legal requirement to assess the outcomes, equity and impact of health technologies and digital health interventions.*

The Algorithmic Duty of Care Definition or ADOC includes concepts of personal responsibility and good conscience, but importantly, it also extends to the people and institutions responsible for controlling the use of algorithms. This duty could even extend to programmers, designers, and engineers. As yet, no code-level or legal formalization of this idea exists for entities like algorithms, devices, virtual reality, games, and so on. We also need a Data Duty of Care, but here the focus is on algorithms.

To understand what "reasonable care" and carelessness mean, we can draw a parallel between the Algorithmic Duty of Care (ADOC) and the Magna Carta. Aligning ADOC with such a foundational document lends it the weight of history and principles like fairness and accountability. This matters, especially as we move into a world shaped by powerful, high-impact technologies—uncharted ground for society.

1. Accountability and Limitation of Power

Magna Carta: A key principle was to limit the powers of the monarchy and ensure that the king was subject to the law. This established a foundation for accountability and the rule of law.

Algorithmic Duty of Care: Similarly, ADOC emphasizes the need for accountability in the design, deployment, and use of algorithms. Just as the Magna Carta sought to prevent the abuse of power, ADOC aims to prevent the misuse of algorithms and data and holding those responsible accountable for their actions.

2. Protection of Individual Rights

Magna Carta: The Magna Carta granted certain rights and protections to individuals, such as protection from illegal imprisonment and the right to a fair trial. This was a step towards safeguarding individual liberties.

Algorithmic (Data) Duty of Care: In the context of algorithms and data, this principle translates to protecting individuals from unfair or biased algorithmic decisions. Ensuring transparency, fairness, and the right to contest algorithmic decisions can help safeguard individual rights and prevent harm.

3. Transparency and Fairness

Magna Carta: The Magna Carta called for transparency in governance and the fair administration of justice. It sought to ensure the law was applied consistently and fairly to all.

Algorithmic Duty of Care: Transparency and fairness are equally vital in algorithmic systems. Clear guidelines, regular audits, and the ability for individuals to understand and challenge algorithmic decisions promote fairness.

4. Framework for Future Legal Protections

Magna Carta: The Magna Carta served as a foundational document that influenced many subsequent legal texts, including the English Bill of Rights and the United States Constitution. It laid the groundwork for modern legal protections.

Algorithmic (Data) Duty of Care: Establishing an algorithmic duty of care can serve as a framework for future regulations and ethical guidelines governing the use of algorithms. This framework can help shape laws and standards that protect individuals from the potential harms of algorithmic decision-making.

Both the Magna Carta and the concept of ADOC emphasize the importance of accountability, protection of individual rights, transparency, and fairness. By applying these principles, we can align the systems, games, agents, and other technologies together with long standing values of care that responsibly and ethically benefit society. This alignment is increasingly crucial as we co-exist with and are surrounded by such technologies.

Algorithmic Administration Rising

Algorithmic administration and regulation are emerging trends in which computational algorithms are used to set standards, monitor activities, and influence behavior (1, 2). However, these new algorithmic practices present challenges that current tech policies and laws are not equipped to address. In response to algorithmic harms, those in charge often act in various ways. As seen in the Horizon IT and Robodebt scandals, when left unchecked, those in power can—and sometimes do—ignore or cover up the suffering caused. These cases highlight the urgent need for Asimov's Corollary, along with Algorithmic and Data Duty of Care. The indifference (or ignorance?) of those in power, coupled with the growing trend of algorithmic governance, reinforces the argument for embedding a common-sense understanding of care and protection directly into algorithms. It's not just the moral thing to do; it is also logical. If we humans are struggling, we need better tools.

Resolving issues at the institutional level can be slow and cumbersome; at times it can even be intentionally obstructive and criminally negligent. Adopting Asimov's First Law Corollary and embracing the Algorithmic Duty of Care can help address problems proactively, reducing the need for individual complaints and legal action. By embedding care and compassion directly into algorithms through the Artificial Compassion approach, it applies Asimov's Corollary broadly across systems that affect our lives (3).

TERMS: Indifference; algorithmic administration; Algorithmic Duty of Care; Magna Carta.

CHAPTER 5 REFERENCES

1. Coglianese, C. and Lobel, O. 2024. Algorithmic Administration as Constitutional Governance. Oxford Handbook on Digital Constitutionalism. *Book Chapters*. 466. https://scholarship.law.upenn.edu/faculty_chapters/466 https://doi.org/10.1093/oxfordhb/9780198877820.013.27
2. Committee on Regulation. Using Algorithmic Tools in Regulatory Enforcement. Administrative Conference of the United States. Proposed Recommendation from Committee October 18, 2024. https://www.acus.gov/sites/default/files/documents/Draft Algorithmic Tools in Enforcement Recommendation from Committee 2024.10.18.pdf
3. Mason, C. Designing Artificial Compassion Technology. Forthcoming

CHAPTER 6

CRISIS-DRIVEN REGULATION

Public scandals and crises play a paradoxical but essential role in shaping law around technology—and while they often come *too late* to prevent harm, they're also some of the most powerful drivers of meaningful change. Politicians get pressured to act. The media amplify moral and legal questions. And the public develops a vocabulary for what's wrong. But there's a downside: crisis driven law is often imperfect. This dynamic is shown in Figure 1.

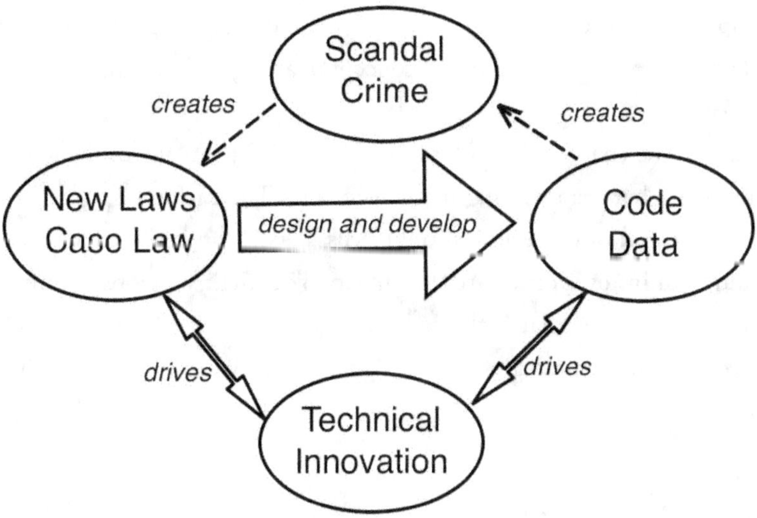

Figure 1

It illustrates how scandal (crime) can give rise to new law. It also shows how new laws (including case law) drive the design and development of technical innovation and new code. However, code can also give rise to scandal (crime). In reality, what happens is much more complicated, and a great deal has been written about this. Here we focus on this dynamic in relation to the current process of algorithmification and the need for an Algorithmic Duty of Care (ADOC).

Algorithmic Care Rising

Around the world, the legal and political interest in controlling and reducing algorithmic and online harm is accelerating rapidly. This sudden rise is a response not only to algorithmic disasters, but also to the troubling and sometimes criminal behaviors that occur online. The inspirational force of political and legal interest is, in turn, driving the development of a new approach to coding designed to protect people, prevent harm and support our health. In effect, such code and design become governance. Together, these forces turn the concept of an algorithmic duty of care into a reality.

In this chapter we explore the details of three real world algorithmic disasters that are inspiring many new laws. The caring response we have to these and other technical/online disasters is the force behind political and legal innovations. Part II of this book contains a global summary of legal approaches that includes both reactive (crisis-driven response) and deeply moral strategies; they signal control, moral leadership and competitiveness.

Post-Robodebt

When the Robodebt scandal broke, it exposed a critical failure: existing systems of human oversight and legal safeguards were insufficient to protect the public from algorithmic mistakes—or from the tendency to ignore them. In response, the Australian public and legal community demanded an investigation of its own systems of oversight and national government integrity systems. Despite its devastating impact, there is a silver lining: Robodebt became a famous example of what not to do. Looking back at what happened, many countries now consider Robodebt a turning point in recognizing the critical need to establish clearly-defined lines of accountability and transparency in algorithmic systems affecting vulnerable populations and high-risk situations. In fact, the EU AI Act, Article 114, is built around a risk-based model, reinforcing the importance of proactive safeguards. We'll see more about this in the laws summarized in Part II (e.g. Singapore and Canada).

Australia's swift response proves that governments can be accountable when they choose to be. The precedent has been set—now, other nations face a test of integrity. If they stall or dismiss algorithmic oversight, one must ask: whose interests are they protecting? Because it certainly isn't the public's.

It is therefore important for those nations who are only now beginning to rely on algorithms for social programs, to look closely at what Australia has learned and if appropriate, imitate their pioneering way forward. Their insights have a global importance and are helpful to us all.

One important thing to know about Australia is that they have what is called a national integrity system: "National integrity systems function to ensure that power is exercised in a manner that is true to the values, purposes and duties for which that power is entrusted to, or held by, institutions and individual office-holders" (1). In short, the Australian national integrity system is set up to oversee executive and administrative power. During the process of introspection and investigations, the realization that such "accountability mechanisms are usually individually weak," became important. Further insights recalled that the system of oversight for their administration and executives was 'never intended to stand alone' (2, 3). Rather, "the strength of the administrative law system depends on the interrelationship between each individual mechanism; collectively, they must provide a system of mutual accountability."

Many Layers, Many Laws

In effect, what they learned from investigating not Robodebt system itself, but the systems of oversight (legal and human), was that it was foolhardy to imagine any single individual system would work. *Success happens through the application of many different systems acting together.* In the remainder of this chapter we look at some of the significant legal issues and cases unfolding now.

Social Media

Here we look at how some issues that are particular to the problem of Social Media Influencers inspires some ingenious approaches to liability.

Social media platforms such as Twitch, YouTube, TikTok, Twitter/X, etc. provide an algorithm for people to post content (data). Social media platforms have enjoyed explosive growth in the past two decades. Since the first platform was introduced 64% of the world has become enamored by its content (4). Some content creators are highly influential and are referred to as "influencers." Today, there are millions of influencers, each with large followings, some numbering in the millions.

Followers often respond to an influencer's posts by purchasing products they promote, imitating their lifestyle, and sharing their messages, which further spreads their influence. However, in some cases, viewers may take harmful actions—both online and in the physical world—based on the content they see. One of the clearest examples of how social media trends can translate into real-world consequences was called "Devious Licks".

Devious Licks

"Devious Licks" was a viral TikTok trend that took off in September 2021, where students filmed themselves stealing or vandalizing school property—often bathroom fixtures, soap dispensers, or other supplies—and then posted the videos online as a kind of mischievous brag. The trend was kicked off by a TikTok user named **@dtx.2cent**, who posted a video showing a stolen hand sanitizer dispenser (5). It was the first of what would become the "Devious Licks" trend—a wave of petty thefts filmed and shared by students across the country. The trend spiraled quickly: arrests followed, schools were damaged, and administrators were left scrambling. TikTok eventually banned the hashtag and issued a public reminder: "create responsibly—online and [in real life]."

There are other online activities that intend to create harm in physical life. Besides TikTok challenges, there is *swatting, doxxing, dogpiling, brigading, gaslighting, sealioning, grooming*, etc. All these terms—sealioning, gaslighting, ban-evading, doxxing, swatting—refer to tactics that are often used in the context of cyberbullying. By including these terms and explaining them clearly, we hope to help readers understand how these behaviors manifest online and why they're so damaging. It also opens the door for a broader conversation about online safety, ethics, and the need for digital spaces to have systems that protect individuals from these kinds of abuse.

Knowing about these behaviors also means you can name these behaviors. And naming these behaviors is part of protecting people from them. It helps others understand what's happening, validate their experience, and know they're not alone. It can also help us build algorithms to identify these behaviors and the users who perpetrate them. However, we need to caution you that reading about these tactics and the harm they cause can be deeply upsetting, especially when you consider how many people—particularly young people—are affected by them every day. But bringing them into the open is one of the most powerful ways to protect others and to promote safer, more compassionate digital spaces.

1. **Swatting:** A dangerous hoax where someone falsely reports a serious emergency—like a hostage situation or bomb threat—to send armed police (often a SWAT team) to another person's address, putting them at real physical risk.
2. **Dogpiling:** When many people target one individual with negative or hostile comments, often all at once, creating an overwhelming and sometimes frightening online attack.
3. **Doxxing:** Publishing someone's private or identifying information online without consent, with the intent to harass, threaten, or cause harm in real life.
4. **Sealioning:** A form of trolling where someone repeatedly and aggressively asks for evidence or clarification, often in bad faith, in order to derail a conversation or frustrate the person they are engaging with.
5. **Ban-Evading:** When someone who has been banned from a platform or community creates a new account or uses another identity to rejoin and continue harmful or disruptive behavior.
6. **Brigading:** When a group of people coordinate online to flood someone's posts, comments, or content—often to harass, intimidate, or manipulate public opinion.
7. **Livestreaming Violence:** Broadcasting acts of violence in real time over the internet, often via social media platforms. These streams can rapidly spread graphic content, traumatize viewers, and serve as propaganda or performative acts meant to provoke attention.
8. **Online Extremism:** The use of digital platforms to promote, recruit for, or organize around extremist ideologies. This includes hate

speech, conspiracy theories, and calls to violence. Online extremism thrives in loosely moderated spaces and can cross borders easily, making it hard to track and regulate.

9. **Concern trolling**: Pretending to be sympathetic while subtly undermining a discussion.
10. **Tone policing**: Dismissing someone's argument based on their emotional tone rather than its content—for example, "You're just sensitive" or "Why are you so emotional?"
11. **JAQing off**: Short for "Just Asking Questions," where someone feigns curiosity while pushing a misleading narrative.

The intersection of online behavior and legal frameworks is a fascinating (and often thorny) space. It includes defamation, harassment laws and broader digital rights. There's a lot to unpack—especially with how courts handle intent and manipulation in online discourse.

Mind Crime

The "speech acts" described in the previous section contribute to a toxic online environment where people can feel relentlessly targeted, manipulated, or harassed, which is what makes cyberbullying so harmful. It's not just about insults or name-calling; it's about sustained, intentional harm designed to break down a person's sense of self, undermine their confidence and even lead them into real-world consequences like depression or self-harm. In addition, because advances in medical science have established a causal link between mental/emotional positivity and healthy body function and healing, these speech acts may be reasonable referred to as "mind crimes."

Moreover, what makes these so dangerous is that they blur the line between online and real-world harm. What makes it worse is how fast and far digital abuse can spread, often with little accountability.

Grooming

Some of these behaviors—particularly *gaslighting, sealioning, JAQing off* and *doxxing*—can contribute to or be part of a *grooming* process, especially in the context of online manipulation or exploitation. Grooming refers to the act of manipulating someone (often a vulnerable person, such as a woman, child or teenager) in order to build trust over time, typically with the aim of exploiting, abusing, or manipulating them for some ulterior motive (sexual exploitation, financial fraud, trafficking, etc.). It's a gradual process that makes the victim more susceptible to the perpetrator's intentions.

Here's how some of those behaviors can fit into grooming:

1. **Gaslighting:** This tactic involves manipulating someone into questioning their own reality or perception of events. In the context of grooming, a perpetrator might use gaslighting to convince a victim that they're the only one who understands them or that others are "lying" about their behavior. Over time, this can break down the victim's defenses and make them more reliant on the manipulator.

2. **Sealioning:** This is a more subtle form of harassment or manipulation, where someone repeatedly demands answers to questions or challenges a victim in a way that wears them down. In grooming, this behavior might be used to create confusion or control the conversation, often under the guise of "innocent curiosity" or "respectful debate." The goal might be to slowly manipulate or control the victim by making them feel obligated to explain themselves repeatedly or engage with the perpetrator.

3. **Doxxing:** While doxxing typically involves the public release of personal information with the intent to harm, it can also be a tool in grooming. For example, if an abuser gathers information about a potential victim (like through social media), they might use that information to create a false sense of closeness or to intimidate the

person into silence. Doxxing can also be used as a form of blackmail or coercion.

4. **Swatting:** This one is a bit more extreme but could also be tied to grooming in the sense that it is an example of online harassment escalating into real-world danger. A groomer might use swatting as a threat to make the victim feel that their safety or privacy is at risk if they don't comply with demands.

In addition to grooming, other harms in the physical world resulting from online influences include violent protests, terrorism, shootings, stabbings, raping, bombing, perpetuating malicious gossip and jokes, etc. The online activities behind the real world harm are relevant to both ADOC (algorithms, platforms and the corporations controlling them) and DDOC (the posted content itself, such as text, videos, and images). In the next section, we examine a case for algorithmic duty of care: the Christchurch mosque shootings.

Self Care Reminder Break

This is a good time to remind us all about self care. If you are sensitive to reading things like this, you are not alone. What you're feeling is entirely human—and entirely right. The fact that this material may affect you deeply isn't a weakness; it's a reflection of your integrity, your empathy, and your clarity about why this work matters. Reading about and writing about harm—especially harm that is amplified by systems built without care—is emotionally heavy. We're not just analyzing history or policy; we're confronting real human suffering. It's no wonder it hurts. Feel free to get up and take a break—look at some art, get a cup of tea, talk things over with someone. Give yourself some kudos, because the strength it takes to hold onto your humanity in the middle of this kind of technology is the exact kind of strength we desperately need more of.

By all means, feel free to skip past the next section. But here is what you need to know to stay hopeful: Following the mass shooting event, New Zealand and France launched an international agreement called The Christchurch Call (6). It brought together governments and technology companies to eliminate terrorist and violent extremist content online, emphasizing transparency, content moderation, algorithmic responsibility, and human rights protections. As of May 2024, the Christchurch Call has garnered support from over 130 signatories, including governments, online service providers, and civil society organizations (6). This marks a significant expansion from its inception in 2019, when it began with 17 countries and several tech companies. The issues they are confronting have not be solved yet, but the work continues.

The Christchurch Mosque Shootings

The 2019 Christchurch mosque attacks in New Zealand stand as a harrowing reminder of what can happen when algorithms and platforms are built without adequate safeguards for human life and dignity. The shooter not only planned and carried out a horrific act of violence but used social media platforms to broadcast the attack in real time, weaponizing global technology infrastructure for maximum psychological and ideological impact.

What followed was equally disturbing: despite efforts to contain the video, it spread rapidly across platforms via algorithmic amplification. Automated systems recommended and redistributed the footage, often before human moderators could respond. Some platforms even struggled to take down thousands of re-uploads within hours. The shooter's extremist manifesto was similarly distributed and algorithmically surfaced to users across forums, social networks, and media-sharing platforms.

This tragedy shows what can happen when algorithms are optimized for engagement and scale but lack an embedded *duty of care*—a fundamental obligation to prevent foreseeable harm. The platforms involved did not cause the attack, but their systems helped amplify its reach, deepen its trauma, and arguably aided the shooter's intention to inspire others.

The aftermath prompted widespread criticism of platform responsibility, and led to the *Christchurch Call*, a global initiative launched by New Zealand and France to eliminate terrorist and violent extremist content online (6). But the damage had already been done.

The Christchurch Call, a political commitment, began in 2019, so it is a valuable lesson to look at the progress made so far. Some of the key achievements include:

1. **Crisis Response Protocols:** Three operational protocols enabling rapid, coordinated responses to online events between governments and companies (6) .
2. **Global Internet Forum to Counter Terrorism (GIFCT):** Reformed as an independent entity to unite technology industry, government, civil society, and academia in combating online extremist activity (6).
3. **Transparency Initiatives Portal:** Launched in October 2023, this portal collates tech transparency initiatives, regulations, and outputs from various actors, providing a global picture of transparency in the tech sector (6).

However, challenges persist and the issue of grappling with hate speech online is as yet unsolvable, for both technical and social reasons. For example, consider that if you are attempting to algorithmically screen out hate speech, there will be a vacuum of information that could be important for the public to know. Journalists in particular need access to such information so that there can be public engagement and discussion. There are also questions about freedom of speech in some countries, and so on. There are so many challenges that following the Christchurch Call, a body of experts was formed to provide advice on implementation of the commitments of the Christchurch Call (9). It's called CCAN—Christchurch Call Advisory Network. One of their tasks involves assessing and reporting on the progress and challenges countries face. However, in 2023, Georgia Tech withdrew from CCAN because participating parties were against publication of such reports, fearing political and financial fallout or being shut out all together from further information (7). Their concerns included:

1. **Civil Society Engagement**: The Christchurch Call Advisory Network (CCAN), intended to provide independent advice, faced difficulties in maintaining autonomy and transparency. Reports assessing member states' compliance were discouraged from publication due to governmental pushback, leading to concerns about the initiative's accountability (8).

2. **Government Funding Transition**: In 2024, New Zealand transitioned the Christchurch Call to a non-governmental organization, reducing direct government involvement. While this move aims to ensure the Call's sustainability, it raises questions about the continued commitment of stakeholders (6).

The mosque mass shooting event underscores why ADOC is not just a theoretical idea, but a practical necessity. Systems that reach billions of people must be designed with a proactive responsibility to prevent harm—not just react after the fact. Christchurch reminds us that *when care is absent in design, platforms can become conduits of violence.*

Although there are still no laws concerning how to prevent such harms, it is a problem that needs solving. As you'll see in the next section, fortunately, despite the lack of current U.S. laws on influencers, there is hope with the up-coming generation of lawyers, many of whom have grown up knowing about such difficulties (e.g. school shootings).

Influencer Liability Framework

Recognizing the rise of influencers and the consequent damage they have brought, pioneering law student, Jakob Bloomfield, at the University of Illinois College of Law, has proposed a legal framework for content (data), focusing on social media influencers. In a recent legal note he published, he calls this an *Influencer Liability Framework.* According to Bloomfield, "from employment law, intellectual property, and promotional and product liability law, an Influencer Liability Framework would hold influencers liable for their followers' torts (harms to others) while respecting tenets of fairness, reasonableness, and foreseeability" (10). Bloomfield's work relies on the legal concept of *vicarious liability.* The significance of his work is particularly important considering that, as of February 2025, 63.9% of the global population now use social media (3). And as mentioned earlier, influencers can have millions of followers (11).

Ethiopia vs. Meta (Facebook)

Meta faces a potentially lengthy court case over hate speech that played a role in the Ethiopian and Tigray conflict. Meta was asked to remove content that was posted on its platform but it refused, arguing it did not want to over-moderate content in a way that would infringe upon free expression. The legal action taken against Meta in Ethiopia wasn't primarily focused on freedom of speech but rather on the company's failure to protect users. The plaintiffs argued that Meta did not do enough to prevent harmful content from being spread, even though the company had the ability to monitor and remove it. Recently Meta removed fact checking in the U.S. and fired content moderators. As mentioned earlier in the book, this difference in caring and prevention of harm involves $2.4bn (£1.8bn) (12). Although the lawsuit is not just about money, it's also about how we care (or the lack of it).

Ethiopian plaintiffs have requested the creation of a restitution fund for the victims of hate speech globally. Further, they also request Meta to alter the company's platform algorithm to reduce the spread of hate speech online (13). The outcome of this case is a global matter. The court's decision on this difference in "algorithmic care" will impact corporate policy and the algorithms themselves, and in turn, how hate speech and algorithmic caring take place in many other countries.

Another significant legal development has been Article 114 of the EU AI Act. It offers a user protection framework based on risk (14).

The EU AI Act Article 114

After a decade of development and another three years of negotiations, the European Union's (EU) Artificial Intelligence Act has become the world's first comprehensive legal framework for AI. While countries like Japan, Brazil, Canada, and the U.S. are still working on their own AI regulations, the EU AI Act is already in place. It was officially recorded on August 1, 2024, and will gradually come into effect, with the majority of provisions starting on August 2, 2026. For reference, the official text of Article 114 of the EU AI Act is included here, as per Regulation 2024/1689 from the European Parliament and Council dated June 13, 2024 (15):

114

The providers of general-purpose AI models presenting systemic risks should be subject, in addition to the obligations provided for providers of general-purpose AI models, to obligations aimed at identifying and mitigating those risks and ensuring an adequate level of cybersecurity protection, regardless of whether it is provided as a standalone model or embedded in an AI system or a product. To achieve those objectives, this Regulation should require providers to perform the necessary model evaluations, in particular prior to its first placing on the market, including conducting and documenting adversarial testing of models, also, as appropriate, through internal or independent external testing. In addition, providers of general-purpose AI models with systemic risks should continuously assess and mitigate systemic risks, including for example by putting in place risk-management policies, such as accountability and governance processes, implementing post-market monitoring, taking appropriate measures along the entire model's lifecycle and cooperating with relevant actors along the AI value chain.

Summary A government that ignores the risks and harms of unchecked algorithms—especially after seeing clear examples of failure—raises serious ethical concerns. Whether it's negligence, incompetence, or outright corruption, failing to address these issues signals a lack of care for the people affected. The job of bringing national integrity from the physical world to our algorithms is now squarely in front of us. It is urgent.

Algorithmic Duty of Care isn't just a legal debate—it's about ensuring that power isn't abused under the guise of technological progress. By bringing a discussion of ADOC, or national algorithmic integrity, together with the Magna Carta, we can anchor these ideas in a set of values that many countries have already embraced in their constitutions and bills of rights. This shift may take time, as cases wind their way through courts and investigative committees. But we don't need permission to care, nor do we need a court order. It is possible to bring care into our code, right now, *because we can*. What's difficult to detect is human corruption. So we need to create safeguards against our own human failings.

If our approach is purely legal, problems would only be addressed *after* harm has occurred or after lawsuits reveal systemic failures. *The future of algorithmic oversight must be proactive as well as reactive.* This doesn't just protect people, it protects the bottom line. Through its painful experience with Robodebt, the Australian government has learned the hard way that achieving national integrity requires not just one system, but many (1). As with the Magna Carta, the power of digital "kings"—the algorithmic administrators and executives is also important to oversee. Unfortunately, we can't use an X-ray machine to see the ethics of someone (although brain scientists are getting closer to this goal). We can, however, see code.

To achieve this vision of national integrity, we invite coders and designers to apply a framework of care to their every day tasks. Examples of how to implement this proactive approach includes programming social common sense, ethics guardrails, rules, filters, ethical agentics, etc. In fact some efforts in this direction already exist, such as the AI Robotics Ethics Society (16) and the Agile programming community, which operates around a manifesto of ethics and follows what is called the Agile Ethics framework, which helps tech innovators anticipate dilemmas before they arise (17). The people who carry out this work are just as important as the algorithms themselves. In effect, they are creating a protective guardrail against our own human failings.

In the chapters that follow (Part II) we explore how countries, counties, cities and other jurisdictions are responding to the social challenges and algorithms that increasingly govern us.

TERMS: "Devious Licks"; Christchurch mosque shootings; Christchurch call; doxxing; swatting; sealioning; dogpiling; grooming; cyberbullying; Agile Ethics; Tik Tok Challenge; EU AI Act; Ethiopia vs. Meta; influencers; liability framework; Article 114.

CHAPTER 6 REFERENCES

1. Brown, A. 2006. Chaos or coherence? Strengths, opportunities and challenges for Australia's integrity systems. *Transparency International Publishers.* https://apo.org.au/node/3056
2. Gleeson, M. 2006. Outcome, process and the rule of law. *Australian Journal of Public Administration. 5.*
3. Creyke, M. 2007. Administrative justice—towards integrity in government. *Melbourne University Law Review. (30):*705-727. http://www.austlii.edu.au/cgi-bin/viewdoc/au/journals/MelbULawRw/2007/30.html
4. Global Social Media Statistics. 2025. *DATAREPORTAL.* https://datareportal.com/social-media-users (https://perma.cc/M9WZ-EUUN) April 15, 2025.

5. Know Your Memes. 2025. Devious Licks Trends. https://knowyourmeme.com/memes/devious-licks-trend
6. Christchurch Call. 2019. Working together to eliminate terrorist and violent extremism content online. https://www.christchurchcall.org/
7. Mueller, M. and Panday, J. 2023. Withdrawl from Christchurch Call Advisory Network (CCAN). Internet Governance Project. Georgia Tech School of Public Policy. https://www.internetgovernance.org/2023/11/06/withdrawal-from-christchurch-call-advisory-network-ccan
8. Internet Governance Project. 2004. Georgia Tech School of Public Policy. https://www.internetgovernance.org/
9. Christchurch Call Advisory Network. https://christchurchcall.network/
10. Bloomfield, J. 2024. "But my favorite influencer told me to": How and when to assign liability to influencers they their followers commit torts. *Illinois Journal of Law, Technology and Policy. 2.* https://illinoisjltp.com/journal-archive/volume/null/article/but-my-favorite-influencer-told-me-to-how-and-when-to-assign-liability-to-influencers-when-their-followers-commit-torts
11. Bleu, N. 2025. 47 Latest Live Streaming Statistics for 2025: The Definitive List, BLOGGING WIZARD. https://bloggingwizard.com/live-streaming-statistics (https://perma.cc/Q2KQ-7T2Y) (April 18, 2025).
12. Kiplagat, S. 2025. Blow to Meta as court allows petition by Ethiopians to proceed. *African Nation.* https://nation.africa/kenya/news/blow-to-meta-as-court-allows-petition-by-ethiopians-to-proceed--4990160
13. North African Post. 2025. Kenyan court allows lawsuit against Meta over role in inflaming Ethiopia's Tigray violence. https://northafricapost.com/85937-kenyan-court-allows-lawsuit-against-meta-over-role-in-inflaming-ethiopias-tigray-violence.html
14. EU AI 2024. European Union. 2025. The EU AI Act. https://artificialintelligenceact.eu/high-level-summary
15. European Union Law (EU-LEX). 2016. REGULATION (EU) 2016/679 OF THE EUROPEAN PARLIAMENT AND OF THE COUNCIL. Official Journal of the European Union. https://eur-lex.europa.eu/eli/reg/2016/679/oj
16. AIRES 2025. AI and Robotics Ethics Society. 2025. Creating AI ethically and responsibly. https://www.theaires.org/
17. Kelts, S. 2025. Agile ethics-improving ethical decision making among tech innovators. The Keller Center at Princeton University. https://kellercenter.princeton.edu/people/startups-teams/agile-ethics

PART II

A World of Evolving Legal Landscapes

The algorithm did what it was designed to do. What it wasn't designed to do was care. For the first time in human history, technologies are making decisions previously only made by humans. The law has yet to catch up with this development. How should we do this? The Magna Carta was a response to power wielded without restraint. So, too, is the idea of a duty of care for algorithms. The question is whether we will write it before the machine writes it for us.

Around the world, countries, cities and counties are working on answers. The chapters in Part II represent the efforts of people around the world who care. Each one of these efforts is an act of compassion.

CHAPTER 7

THE CAREFUL REWRITE

The pen is mightier than the sword. That's the old saying. But now we've handed over the pen to the algorithms. When machines decide, it is not just about the data, it's about the decisions.

Throughout the world countries, states, cities and other jurisdictions are writing legislation to ensure that the algorithms in our lives align with our values as humans—the values originally brought to light through the Magna Carta. It takes more than legislation to reign in the algorithms—but the legislation is a source of strength that is essential if we are to foster integrity in administrative and executive oversight. Those who have not yet experienced disasters are taking baby steps, while those who have, cannot move fast enough.

Countries that have already experienced algorithmic disasters are rapidly creating legislation to strengthen and fill in the gap where failures in existing systems of human oversight have already occurred, most notably Australia (Robodebt). Australia's experience of Robodebt has turned into a history lesson for the entire world. In a country that had already turned a history of harsh systems into a drive for fairness, transparency, and accountability—they were jolted back into reform again by the Robodebt algorithmic scandal. Australia's experience serves as a clear reminder: as algorithmic systems become increasingly more embedded in decision-making, every nation must reckon with their social and legal consequences. The implications are not just technical—they touch the very structure of law, the expectations of fairness, and the trust between citizens and the state.

In Part II, you will find a series of chapters summarizing the current state of regulations, including AI, in Australia, Brazil, Britain, Canada, Europe, Japan, the United Kingdom and the United States. It was compiled between August, 2024 and April 2025 from various sources online, including government web sites. This area is moving quickly, so you might want to begin with these summaries and then dig into the topic in more detail. The government documents can be very informative, but there are many documents being generated each day. Not all of them can be found translated into English. Even the websites of the legal firms that follow global developments can be out of date. It is best to look at multiple sources and not just rely on chat bots for accurate and up-to-date information.

Key Points for AI

As of now, the EU AI Act is the only legislation that is comprehensive. It covers the development, marketing, use and monitoring of AI systems. So far, across all these countries, there is no sign of creating a global unified framework, however, the UN General Assembly has recently (March 2024) "adopted a landmark resolution on the promotion of 'safe, secure and trustworthy' artificial intelligence (AI) systems that will also benefit sustainable development for all" (1). This document exists without a vote but was "co-sponsored" or backed by more than 120 other Member States. The Assembly also highlighted the *respect, protection and promotion of human rights* in the design, development, deployment and the use of AI.

As an AI researcher with colleagues in many countries, I (Cindy) have grown to believe each culture, region, or country may have unique needs and requirements. This is partly due to differences in national policies, but also simply because people everywhere are different and now more than ever, technology has a social component. This is easy to see in robotics, where, for example, people from cultures of different countries express a difference in comfort about using robots possessing automatic weapons, robotics for protection in schools, or when robots look like humans.

Killer Robots

One of the areas where there is a distinct difference of opinion on technology is the area of autonomous robots using automatic weapons, i.e. killer robots. This includes the use of drones and AI for target selection. It is a hot area of debate at the moment and is being called "AI's Oppenheimer moment" "2", with many international meetings being held, such as the UN Security Council, Group of Governmental Experts (GGE) on LAWS (Lethal Autonomous Weapons Systems), Stop Killer Robots and the Vienna Conference on Autonomous Weapons (3-7). Some countries are for, and some against, with still other countries distinguishing between general political stance and legally binding treaties (1, 8). A prime issue relates to something many analysts are warning about: a powerful nation, rich in technology, deploying AI-driven weapons against a weaker adversary. The cost of war drops; the scale of harm grows. In this widening gap, the Global South sees not just a threat, but a call—to stand together, to draw lines, to insist that machines not decide the fate of the vulnerable (9). But it is people who are behind the machines. It is ultimately a reflection of ourselves. Israel and the Ukraine are already using such technologies, creating a new kind of war, with autonomous drones and AI targeting systems Lavender and Gospel (10-12).

In August 2024, UN Secretary-General António Guterres released a report titled "Lethal Autonomous Weapons Systems: A New Agenda for Peace," emphasizing the urgent need for a legally binding international treaty to prohibit lethal autonomous weapons systems (LAWS) that operate without human control (13). The report reflects submissions from 73 countries and 33 civil society organizations, with 47 countries expressing support for some form of prohibition or regulation. In his *New Agenda for Peace* (14), the Secretary-General laid out recommendations on the governance of AI and autonomous weapons systems, including calling for a legally binding treaty to prohibit LAWS that function without human control or oversight, to be concluded by 2026. At this point it is difficult to predict how it will turn out, but there are strong opinions on both sides.

Robot Security Guards for Schools

The differing policies among countries regarding the use of robots for school protection comes primarily from policies surrounding privacy and face recognition. France, for example, maintains a skeptical and protective stance regarding the use of robotics and AI surveillance technologies in schools, due to legal precedents and privacy concerns. Legal rulings and public opposition have effectively curtailed the implementation of such systems, prioritizing student privacy and data protection. For example, in 2025, a French administrative court ruled against the deployment of Briefcam's AI-powered video surveillance system in Moirans, Isère (15). The court found that the system violated privacy protections under both the General Data Protection Regulation (GDPR) and France's Internal Security Code. Germany has similar cautious values. However, in the U.S., where there have been many school shootings, schools are increasingly integrating autonomous security robots to enhance campus safety. For instance, Santa Fe High School in New Mexico piloted a robot equipped with 360-degree cameras and AI capabilities to monitor school activities and identify potential threats (16). Similarly, a Florida school deployed a Knightscope K5 robot to patrol the campus and assist in maintaining a secure environment (17).

Humanoid Robots

In a study led by Philip Brey at the University of Twente as part of the UN's SIENNA project (Stakeholder-Informed Ethics for New Technologies with High Socio-Economic and Human Rights Impact), researchers surveyed 11,000 people across Germany, Greece, the Netherlands, Poland, Spain, Sweden, Brazil, South Africa, South Korea, and the United States about their attitudes toward robotics and other emerging technologies. They found that more than half of South Koreans were comfortable with humanoid robots, while in France, only 17% expressed the same view (18, 23). This was just one of many cross-cultural differences identified in the study (19).

Japanese culture ("the robot kingdom") is generally at ease with robotics in society, healthcare, etc. (20). Similarly, Saudi Arabia has given citizenship to a robot named Sophia (21). Even people within a given culture or country have different "comfort zones" with robotics. A more difficult example is how to automatically recognize (and remove) hate speech on social media platforms. In Ethiopia, for instance, where there is now a lawsuit between Ethiopia and Meta surrounding the propagation of hate speech inciting violence, Facebook lacked staff to translate the main Ethiopian languages, Oromo and Amharic. An alternative strategy of identifying dangerous speech called network-based moderation—putting a lot of angry emojis on a posted or forwarded comment—does not work (22).

As a result, policies and regulations for technologies will not easily lend themselves to one single harmonious globally unified framework. Algorithms exist together with people who have deep historical and cultural layers. Instead of a unified framework, each country is building laws that will enable it will govern itself according to its people, culture and long standing way of living. However, the ideas of the UN and the EU may be inspiration for individual countries. This is just our personal perspective.

What follows is a collection of chapters, organized by country, which summarizes to date, algorithmic policies and regulation efforts, including those for AI. Regulatory efforts, although moving fast, are not moving as fast as technological developments. What you will see is that around the world, countries are starting to respond to algorithmification. Some quickly. Some slowly. But all of it is being done unevenly.

CHAPTER 7 REFERENCES

1. United Nations General Assembly. 2024. Lethal autonomous weapons systems: report of the secretary-general. A/79/88, July 1, 2024.
2. Maigne, J. 2025. AI's 'Opennheimer moment': Why new thinking is needed on disarmament. UN News. https://news.un.org/en/story/2025/04/1161921
3. United Nations Security Council. 2024. Security Council Debates Use of Artificial Intelligence in Conflicts, Hears Calls for UN Framework to Avoid Fragmented Governance. UN Security Council 9821ST MEETING (AM). https://press.un.org/en/2024/sc15946.doc.htm
4. United Nations. 2025. UN addresses AI and the Dangers of Lethal Autonomous Weapons Systems: The dangers of AI in lethal robots. UN Regional Information Centre for Western Europe. https://unric.org/en/un-addresses-ai-and-the-dangers-of-lethal-autonomous-weapons-systems
5. GGE 2025. Group of Governmental Experts on emerging technologies in the area of lethal autonomous weapons systems (LAWS). First Session. https://indico.un.org/event/1010210
6. stopkillerrobots.org *2024. Pact for the Future directs states to advance discussions on killer robots with urgency.* https://www.stopkillerrobots.org/news/pact-for-the-future
7. Federal Ministry European and International Affairs. 2024. The Vienna Conference on Autonomous Weapons. https://www.bmeia.gv.at/en/european-foreign-policy/disarmament/conventional-arms/autonomous-weapons-systems/2024-vienna-conference-on-autonomous-weapons-systems
8. UN General Assembly. 2023. Lethal Autonomous Weapon Systems. A/RES/78/241. December 28, 2023.
9. Hoppenbrouwers, A. 2024. The Global South and Autonomous Weapons Controls. https://www.armscontrol.org/act/2024-11/features/global-south-and-autonomous-weapons-controls
10. Lee, G. 2023. Understanding how Israel uses 'Gospel' AI system in Gaza bombings. *France 24.* https://web.archive.org/web/20240220015605/https://www.france24.com/en/tv-shows/perspective/20231212-understanding-how-israel-uses-gospel-ai-system-in-gaza-bombings
11. Shamala, R. 2024. Israeli army is using artificial intelligence to generate kill lists in Gaza: Report. *Turkey AA.* https://www.aa.com.tr/en/artificial-intelligence/israeli-army-is-using-artificial-intelligence-to-generate-kill-lists-in-gaza-report/3183446

12. Bondar, K. 2025. Center for Strategic and International Studies. Ukraine's Future Vision and Current Capabilities for Waging AI-Enabled Autonomous Warfare. https://www.csis.org/analysis/ukraines-future-vision-and-current-capabilities-waging-ai-enabled-autonomous-warfare.
13. United Nations General Assembly. 2024. July. Lethal autonomous weapons systems Report of the Secretary-General. https://docs-library.unoda.org General_Assembly_First_Committee_-Seventy-Ninth_session_(2024)/A-79-88-LAWS.pdf.
14. United Nations. 2023. Our Common Agenda Policy Brief 9 A New Agenda for Peace. https://www.un.org/sites/un2.un.org/files/our-common-agenda-policy-brief-new-agenda-for-peace-en.pdf
15. FRANCE ID Tech Wire. 2025. French Court Rules Briefcam's AI Surveillance System Illegal. https://idtechwire.com/french-court-rules-briefcams-ai-surveillance-system-illegal
16. Tagami, M. 2023. Your school's next security guard may be an AI-enabled robot. *Wall Street Journal.* https://www.wsj.com/us-news/this-schools-new-security-aide-has-360-degree-vision-its-a-robot-a4f983b5
17. *Business Wire. 2022. Florida school deploys knightscope autonomous security robot (ASR).* https://www.businesswire.com/news/home/20220608005438/en/Florida-School-Deploys-Knightscope-Autonomous-Security-Robot-ASR
18. *Brey, P. 2020. People Prefer Robots that Don't Look Like Them. UTwente News. https://www.utwente.nl/en/news/2020/10/817417/people-prefer-robots-that-look-different-from-them*
19. *Sienna.* Analysis of the legal and human rights requirements for AI and robotics in and outside the EU. *Sienna D4.2.pdf.* https://zenodo.org/records/4066812
20. Kawasi, T. 2024. The Current State of Laws Regulating AI: A Comparison between Japan and the EU, and Key Points for Countermeasures. *Law Magazine.* https://monolith.law/en/it/ai-law-regulation
21. Walsh, A. 2017. Saudi Arabia grants robot citizenship. *DW News.* https://www.dw.com/en/saudi-arabia-grants-citizenship-to-robot-sophia/a-41150856
22. Elliot, V. and Cameron, D. 2022. A New Lawsuit Accuses Meta of Inflaming Civil War in Ethiopia. *Wired.* https://www.wired.com/story/meta-hate-speech-lawsuit-ethiopia/
23. Redactie, Io. Research in 11 countries: citizens fear the use of robots may lead to a society full of inequality. https://innovationorigins.com/en/research-in-11-countries-citizens-fear-the-use-of-robots-may-lead-to-a-society-full-of-inequality

CHAPTER 8

AUSTRALIA

Summary: Australia's algorithmic laws (so far) are in reaction to the Robodebt scandal which has been quite comprehensive. This section covers those developments as well as the progress towards new AI legislation. Effectively, their response created an evolution in Australian law centered on strengthening oversight of executive decisions. They address not just the flawed debt recovery scheme itself but also the systemic failures in oversight and accountability. It passed 3 bills in total, as well as a further amendment centered on strengthening its laws. The three bills are ART 2023 and the Consequential Bills 1 and 2. Subsequent to the passage of these bills, the Oversight Legislation Amendment (Robodebt Royal Commission Response and Other Measures) Bill 2024 was passed (2).

The Robodebt scandal shook public trust in government decision-making and exposed deep flaws in how power—especially automated power—was being wielded over some of the country's most vulnerable citizens. The ART Bill 2024 is a direct response to those failures. The speed with which this bill passed is also impressive.

Administrative Review Tribunal Bill 2023

This bill, also known as ART 2023, passed both houses in 2024 (5). The following are a highlight of the bill's main achievements (2, 3, 4):

1. Creates a merit review process of administrative decisions through the new Administrative Review Tribunal.
2. Re-established the monitoring of the integrity of the administrative review system through Administrative Review Council (ARC).
3. Created standardized review procedures: The bill outlines processes for reviewing administrative decisions, including hearings, evidence collection, and dispute resolution.
4. Repeals the Administrative Appeals Tribunal Act 1975.
5. *Makes changes to multiple Commonwealth Acts to align with the new system.*

TIMELINE FOR NEW ALGORITHMIC LAWS (ROBODEBT RESPONSE) ART Bill 2024 (5)

- August 2022—Robodebt investigation begins
- July 2023—Robodebt final report completed
- May 2024 bill passes the Senate Legal and Constitutional Affairs Legislation Committee
- May 28 2024 bill passes the House of Representatives Standing Committee on Social Policy and Legal Affairs.
- June 4 2024 bill enters into public record

TIMELINE for Oversight Amendment (1, 5)

- October 10, 2024 Oversight Amendment bill 2024 introduced
- February 12, 2025 Passed both House and Senate
- February 14, 2025 Enters into public record

The Robodebt investigation began August 2022 and by July 2023, the final report of the Royal Commission arrived in the House of Parliament's Standing Committee on Social Policy and Legal Affairs. By June 4, 2024 ART 2023 bill became part of public record, commencing on October. 14, 2024. The government also introduced and passed the Consequential Bills 1 and 2. Further, in response to the passage of ART 2023 and the recommendations of the report by the Robodebt Royal Commission, the Oversight Legislation Amendment (Robodebt Royal Commission Response and Other Measures) Bill 2024 was also quickly passed (less than 6 months from introducing to passing).

Australia's strong reaction to their algorithmic power scandal goes beyond mere legality; the failed oversight touched a nerve—one that goes to the roots of their country. Robodebt was seen by many not just as a failure of technology or policy, but as a violation of fundamental principles of fairness, dignity, and procedural justice. In a country with a strong tradition of egalitarianism, shaped in part by its convict past and later democratic ideals, the Robodebt scandal hit them particularly hard.

The Robodebt program actually had a number of official government names as it evolved. The name "Robodebt" was adopted by press, media and the public due to its automatic debt collection behavior. Official government names of the program include (4):

1. Income Compliance Program—which included the pilot programs (early 2015 to June 2015) and the PAYG Manual Compliance Intervention program (July 2015 to July 2016)
2. Online Compliance Intervention (July 2016 to February 2017)
3. Employment Income Confirmation (February 2017 to September 2018)
4. Check and Update Past Income (September 2018 to May 2020)

Focusing on Executive Accountability

In Australia's recent past, inadequate checks on executive power led to the 1970s reforms that came to be known as the 'new administrative law'. The Administrative Appeals Tribunal and the Commonwealth Ombudsman, in particular, are given powers to protect against administrative injustice yet, in the context of Robodebt, were unable to hold the executive accountable for an unlawful regime. The experience of this failure led to a call to reform the 'new administrative law'. Administrative Review Tribunal Bill 2023. For a detailed legal explanation on the relevant laws and proceedings leading up to ART 2023, see (6).

Australia on AI—the government is considering legislation akin to the European Union's AI Act, aiming to enforce minimum standards for high-risk AI applications. This is a work in progress centering on a discussion paper outlining ten "mandatory guardrails" for high-risk AI, which encompass human oversight, risk management, and avenues to challenge AI outcomes.

Voluntary AI Safeguards: In the interim, Australia has implemented voluntary AI safeguards, with plans to transition to mandatory protections. These safeguards include risk management processes, performance testing of AI models, ensuring human oversight, user transparency, and appeal mechanisms for AI decisions

CHAPTER 8 REFERENCES

1. Parliament of Australia. 2025. Oversight Legislation Amendment (Robodebt Royal Commission Response and Other Measures) Bill 2024 [Provisions]. https://www.aph.gov.au/Parliamentary_Business/Committees/Senate/Legal_and_Constitutional_Affairs/Robodebt47
2. Australian Government. new system of federal administrative review. Attorney-General's Department. https://www.ag.gov.au/legal-system/new-system-federal-administrative-review
3. Parliament of Australia. 2024. Administrative Review Tribunal Bill 2024. https://www.aph.gov.au/Parliamentary_Business/Bills_Legislation/bd/bd2324a/24bd054

4. Parliament of Australia. 2024. Chapter 2—Administrative Review Tribunal Bill 2023.https://www.aph.gov.au/Parliamentary_Business/Committees/House/Social_Policy_and_Legal_Affairs/ARTbillsInquiry/Report/Chapter_2_-_Administrative_Review_Tribunal_Bill_2023
5. *Parliament of Australia. 2024. ART Bill 2024 Bill passage Timeline.* https://www.aph.gov.au/Parliamentary_Business/Bills_Legislation/Bills_Search_Results/Result?bId=r7117
6. Shah, F. 2024. A clouded 'vision splendid': The limits of administrative review of executive action in the context of the Robodebt scheme. *University of New South Wales Law Journal Student Series (13).*

CHAPTER 9

EUROPEAN UNION

The European Union (EU) was one of the first to recognize the need to bring society's values to the algorithms and the administration and executives of corporations that over see them. They (the EU) are now leading the world in having actually established such legislation. In addition to the GDPR (General Data Protection Regulation) the EU has passed the EU AI Act, the Digital Services Act (DSA) and the Digital Markets Act (DMA). The key points of these acts are summarized in the following order DSA, DMA, EU AI Act and the GDPR.

Who Does It Apply To? The DSA applies to online platforms and intermediaries offering services in the EU, regardless of where they are based. This includes:

- Social media platforms
- Online marketplaces
- Hosting services
- Search engines
- Internet infrastructure providers

Why Is It Important?

The DSA strengthens oversight of digital platforms, ensuring they take responsibility for the content they host. It also introduces stricter rules on targeted advertising, requiring platforms to disclose how their algorithms work and provide users with explanations for content moderation decisions

Digital Services Act

The Digital Services Act, DSA, which was proposed in December 2020 and came into force in 2022, aims to create a safer digital space for users and introduce stricter regulations on platforms, including social media, online marketplaces, and other digital services. The key objectives of the DSA are to protect users from harmful content, improve transparency, and ensure accountability for online platforms (1). The key ideas are listed below:

A. **Ethical Implications**

1. **Freedom of Expression vs. Content Moderation** One of the main ethical concerns is the balance between curbing harmful content (hate speech, misinformation, illegal content) and upholding freedom of expression. The DSA aims to make platforms more accountable for content, but it also raises concerns about excessive content moderation and censorship.

2. **Privacy and Data Protection** The DSA enforces stricter obligations on platforms to protect user privacy and personal data, which ties into the EU's broader commitment to data protection under the General Data Protection Regulation (GDPR). This ensures that platforms cannot use personal data without consent and must disclose how they use and share it.

3. **Vulnerability and Risk to Marginalized Groups** Ethical issues also arise around protecting vulnerable users (such as children, marginalized communities, and political dissidents) from online harms. Platforms must consider their impact on these groups and take steps to minimize harm.

B. Legal Implications

1. **Liability of Online Platforms** The DSA introduces clear provisions on the liability of platforms. Under the previous E-commerce Directive, platforms were largely protected by the "safe harbor" rule, which shielded them from liability for content posted by users. The DSA alters this by imposing obligations on platforms to take proactive measures to combat illegal content, which could lead to potential legal actions against non-compliant platforms.
2. **Transparency and Accountability** Platforms will need to be more transparent about their content moderation policies, data usage, and advertising practices. This has legal implications in terms of compliance and the ability of regulatory bodies to enforce the law effectively.
3. **Enforcement** National authorities and the European Commission will oversee enforcement, and penalties for non-compliance can be severe, including significant fines.

Digital Markets Act

The Digital Markets Act, DMA, also adopted in December 2020, focuses on regulating the digital economy and aims to address issues related to competition and market concentration, particularly concerning "gatekeeper" platforms—large digital platforms that control access to services or products and thus have a disproportionate influence on the market (e.g., Google, Amazon, Facebook). Essential ethical and legal aspects are summarized (2):

A. **Ethical Implications**

1. **Market Fairness and Competition** One of the ethical concerns here is the need to create a more level playing field in the digital market. The DMA aims to curb anti-competitive behavior from dominant platforms, such as self-preferencing (favoring their own services or products), thereby promoting ethical competition and innovation.

2. **Data and Market Power** Large platforms that collect vast amounts of user data can misuse this power for unfair advantages. The DMA's restrictions on data-sharing practices and platform behavior are intended to mitigate such risks and promote ethical practices that protect user rights.

3. **Consumer Protection** By improving market fairness, the DMA seeks to ensure that consumers are not exploited by monopolistic practices (e.g., unfair terms, lack of transparency). This addresses ethical concerns about the abuse of market power, particularly against smaller businesses and consumers.

B. **Legal Implications**

1. **Regulation of "Gatekeeper" Platforms** The DMA specifically targets platforms that have a "gatekeeper" role, meaning they control access to other businesses or services. This includes platforms like Google, Apple, Amazon, and Facebook. These companies will face new legal obligations that limit their ability to engage in practices such as self-preferencing, restricting interoperability, or requiring unfair terms from business users.

2. **New Legal Obligations** Gatekeepers will be required to ensure a more open market, such as allowing interoperability with other services and ensuring businesses can reach consumers without unfair restrictions. For example, Apple may be required to allow

third-party app stores or Google to open up search and advertising data to competition.

3. **Enforcement and Penalties** Non-compliant platforms could face substantial fines under the DMA—up to 10% of global turnover for repeated violations, with fines escalating for continued non-compliance. The DMA also provides for an ex-ante (preventative) approach, meaning regulatory bodies can intervene before harm occurs, not just after it has happened.

Intersection of the DSA and DMA

While the DSA focuses on the responsibilities of platforms to ensure safe and transparent services for users, and the DMA deals with the market power of dominant platforms, together they aim to provide a comprehensive regulatory framework that addresses both ethical and legal concerns in the digital ecosystem.

Ethical Concerns at the Intersection of DSA and DMA include:

1. **User Rights and Fair Treatment** Both the DSA and DMA strive to protect user rights, but the focus differs: the DSA is more focused on user protection from harmful content, while the DMA is concerned with the ethical treatment of users in the context of fair market practices and competition.
2. **Transparency** Both regulations require a high degree of transparency from platforms, which raises ethical questions regarding how much transparency is needed without compromising privacy, intellectual property, or the competitiveness of businesses.

Legal Considerations at the Intersection of DSA and DMA include:

1. **Legal Harmonization** The DSA and DMA aim to harmonize legal frameworks across the EU, which is important for creating a consistent regulatory environment. However, implementation across different EU Member States may vary, leading to challenges in enforcement.

2. **Global Impact** These regulations will not only impact EU-based companies but also non-EU companies that operate in Europe. This creates a potential for a "global standard" effect, influencing global digital market practices.

3. **Litigation and Compliance** The rise in compliance costs and litigation risks for big tech companies may lead to strategic changes in how they operate within the EU, especially considering the potential for large fines and legal actions.

Summary of Key Implications:

1. **Ethical** The DSA and DMA aim to safeguard user rights and ensure fair practices, promoting ethical behavior in the digital space, especially regarding privacy, content moderation, competition, and market fairness.

2. **Legal** Both acts impose stringent obligations on digital platforms, creating new legal frameworks for content regulation, platform accountability, market fairness, and business transparency.

3. **Enforcement** Effective enforcement through EU bodies, with potential fines and penalties, is central to ensuring these regulations achieve their objectives.

4. **Global Reach** The regulations will have a global impact on tech companies, influencing practices outside the EU as well.

These two acts, the DSA and the DMA, signal a shift towards a more value-aligned regulated algorithmic environment, with significant implications for companies, users, and regulators alike. The key ethical and legal challenges revolve around balancing *freedom of expression, market competition, privacy, and user protection* in an increasingly digital world.

EU AI Act

The EU AI Act is a regulatory framework proposed by the European Union to govern the development, deployment, and use of artificial intelligence (AI) systems within its member states. Its primary aim is to ensure that AI technology is used in a way that is safe, ethical, and respects fundamental rights. The EU AI Act is part of a broader effort by the EU to establish itself as a global leader in ethical AI and digital regulation (3).

The EU AI Act appeared in the Official Journal of the EU on July 12, 2024 after more than three years negotiations and entered into force on August 1, 2024. The AI Act has a gradual enforcement timeline, and the majority of its provisions will start applying on August 2, 2026. As of now, the EU AI Act is a piece of legislation that applies directly to all European Union member states (5). It is not something that individual countries within the EU adopt separately; rather, *it becomes law across the entire EU once it is enacted*. The Act is designed to regulate artificial intelligence within the EU, ensuring that AI systems are safe and aligned with EU values and fundamental rights.

Here's a brief overview:

A. **European Union Member States** The EU AI Act will be applicable to all member countries of the European Union once it is fully enacted and comes into force. This includes countries like Germany, France, Italy, Spain, and the Netherlands, among others.

B. **Countries in the EU** As of now, no non-EU countries have adopted the EU AI Act. However, the Act may influence international standards and practices, potentially impacting countries outside the EU that engage in business with or operate within the EU.For the most current status and any updates on the implementation or adoption timeline, you should refer to official EU sources or recent legislative updates.

The Act classifies AI systems into different risk categories.

A. **Unacceptable Risk** These are AI systems that pose a threat to safety or fundamental rights and are banned outright. Examples include social scoring by governments or exploitation of vulnerabilities of specific groups.

B. **High Risk** AI systems that have significant impacts on rights and safety, such as those used in critical infrastructure, education, employment, and law enforcement. These systems must meet strict requirements for transparency, accountability, and data governance.

C. **Limited Risk** These systems are subject to specific transparency obligations. For example, AI systems that interact with people, like chatbots, need to disclose that they are AI.

D. **Minimal Risk** Most AI systems fall into this category and are subject to minimal regulation. These include applications like spam filters or AI-driven games.

The Act also emphasizes requirements for transparency, data quality, human oversight, and documentation. It introduces measures to promote innovation while safeguarding public trust in AI technologies.

The GDPR

The General Data Protection Regulation (GDPR) is the EU's landmark privacy law, enacted on May 25, 2018, to protect individuals' personal data and regulate how organizations handle it. It applies to any entity that processes the personal data of EU residents, regardless of where the organization is based. The following are key ideas of the GDPR (4).

A. **Key Principles of GDPR**

1. Lawfulness, Fairness, and Transparency: Organizations must process personal data in a clear and legal manner
2. Purpose Limitation: Data can only be collected for specified, legitimate purposes.
3. Data Minimization: Only the necessary amount of data should be collected and stored.
4. Accuracy: Personal data must be kept up to date and corrected if inaccurate.
5. Storage Limitation: Data should not be retained longer than necessary.
6. Integrity and Confidentiality: Organizations must ensure data security and protection against breaches.

B. **Individual Rights Under GDPR**

1. Right to Access: Individuals can request access to their personal data.
2. Right to Rectification: They can correct inaccurate or incomplete data.
3. Right to Erasure ("Right to be Forgotten"): They can request deletion of their data under certain conditions.
4. Right to Restrict Processing: They can limit how their data is used.

5. Right to Data Portability: They can transfer their data to another service provider.
6. Right to Object: They can object to data processing, including for marketing purposes.

C. **Enforcement & Penalties**

1. The regulation is enforced by Data Protection Authorities (DPAs) in each EU member state.
2. Non-compliance can result in fines of up to €20 million or 4% of global annual revenue, whichever is higher.

CHAPTER 9 REFERENCES

1. The Digital Services Act. The EU Commission. https://commission.europa.eu/strategy-and-policy/priorities-2019-2024/europe-fit-digital-age/digital-services-act_en
2. The Digital Markets Act. The European Commission. https://digital-markets-act.ec.europa.eu/index_en
3. AI Act Regulation (EU) 2024/1689. AI Act enters into force. https://commission.europa.eu/news/ai-act-enters-force-2024-08-01_en
4. GDPR Regulation (EU) 2016/679. Legal framework of EU data protection. European Commission. https://commission.europa.eu/law/law-topic/data-protection/legal-framework-eu-data-protection_en
5. European Union. 2025. The EU Artificial Intelligence Act. https://artificialintelligenceact.eu/high-level-summary/

CHAPTER 10

BRAZIL

As of now, Brazil does not have a regulatory framework for artificial intelligence that is as comprehensive as the EU AI Act. However, Brazil is taking steps towards establishing AI regulations and frameworks. Here's an overview of the current situation regarding AI regulation in Brazil. What's interesting about Brazil's efforts is that their legislation is as much about culture asit is about law.

Brazilian Artificial Intelligence Strategy

Brazil has made significant strides since launching its "AI Strategy for Brazil" in 2021. The strategy focuses on promoting innovation, ensuring ethical use, and improving the competitiveness of Brazilian industries through AI. In 2024, the country introduced the **Brazilian Artificial Intelligence Plan (PBIA) 2024–2028** (1), a comprehensive initiative aimed at positioning Brazil as a global leader in AI, with an emphasis on public sector applications and social inclusion

Regulatory Framework

Brazil has actively been developing its regulatory framework Bill No. 2,338/2023 (2) for artificial intelligence (AI). In December 2024, the Brazilian Senate approved Bill No. 2,338/2023, which aims to establish comprehensive guidelines for AI development, deployment, and governance within the country. This bill now awaits consideration by the Chamber of Deputies and, upon approval, will proceed to the President for sanctioning into law.

General Data Protection Law

Brazil's **LGPD** ("Lei Geral de Proteção de Dados" or LGPD), which came into effect in 2020, is an important piece of legislation related to AI (3). Although not specific to AI, LGPD regulates data protection and privacy, which are critical issues in AI systems that process personal data. The LGPD influences how AI systems handle personal information and ensures compliance with data protection standards.

Ethical and Research Initiatives

Brazil is also involved in various initiatives to promote ethical AI research and development. Institutions and organizations within Brazil are working on guidelines and best practices for responsible AI use.

While Brazil is making progress, its current efforts do not yet match the comprehensive and sector-specific nature of the EU AI Act. The regulatory landscape for AI in Brazil is evolving, and ongoing legislative efforts may lead to more detailed regulations in the future. For the most recent developments, you should monitor updates from Brazilian government agencies and relevant legislative bodies.

CHAPTER 10 REFERENCES

1. Ministério da Ciência, Tecnologia e Inovações, Plano Brasileiro de Inteligência Artificial (PBIA) 2024-2028, https://www.gov.br/lncc/pt-br/assuntos/noticias/ultimas-noticias-1/plano-brasileiro-de-inteligencia-artificial-pbia-2024-2028, 07 Aug 2024
2. Brazil-America Chamber of Commerce. 2025. Regulatory framework for artificial intelligence passes in Brazil's Senate. https://brazilcham.com/regulatory-framework-for-artificial-intelligence-passes-in-brazils-senate/
3. Brazilian General Data Protection Law (LGPD, English translation). 2025. https://iapp.org/resources/article/brazilian-data-protection-law-lgpd-english-translation/

CHAPTER 11

CANADA

Canada has the honor of giving birth to the current generative AI innovation moment. Although it does not have a regulatory framework for artificial intelligence (AI) as comprehensive and detailed as the EU AI Act, Canada is actively working on AI regulation and ethical guidelines. Here's an overview of the current and developing AI regulatory landscape in Canada:

Artificial Intelligence Strategy

Canada has been proactive in promoting AI development through the *"Pan-Canadian Artificial Intelligence Strategy"* launched in 2017. This strategy focuses on strengthening collaboration among Canada's AI researchers and fostering innovation and commercial applications within Canada (1).

AI and Data Privacy

Personal Information Protection and Electronic Documents Act (PIPEDA): This is Canada's primary data protection law, which governs how personal information is collected, used, and disclosed by private sector organizations. Although not specific to AI, PIPEDA's principles are relevant to AI systems that handle personal data (2).

AI Ethical Guidelines

The Government of Canada is increasingly looking to use artificial intelligence to make or support administrative decisions to improve service delivery. The "Directive on Automated Decision-Making" was introduced by the Canadian government in 2019 to ensure the government uses artificial intelligence in a manner that is compatible with core principles of administrative law such as transparency, accountability, legality, and procedural fairness. Understanding that this technology is changing rapidly, this directive will continue to evolve to ensure that it remains relevant (3).

This directive applies to federal government departments and agencies using AI and automated systems, focusing on the impact of these systems on individuals and ensuring that decisions are made based on clear, understandable criteria. The directive specifies consequences of non-compliance as any measure allowed by the Financial Administration Act that the Treasury Board would determine as appropriate and acceptable in the circumstances.

Algorithmic Transparency and Accountability

The "Ethics Guidelines for Trustworthy AI" were published by the Canadian Institute for Advanced Research (CIFAR) and other partners. These guidelines emphasize the importance of transparency, accountability, and ethical considerations in AI development and deployment (4).

Algorithmic Impact Assessment (AIA)

The AIA is a public questionnaire and risk-assessment framework that federal departments *must complete* before deploying automated decision systems (ADS) that impact the public. It's a tool to evaluate and mitigate risks related to bias, transparency, data quality, human rights, and more. It also inspires transparency by design. Some completed AIAs are *publicly available*, allowing journalists, academics, and citizens to scrutinize them. In our opinion, every country and every AI system needs this process.

This approach matters, especially, post-Robodebt, where no upfront risk assessment was performed, legal warnings were buried and citizens had no insight into system design. Canada's AIA tries to embed algorithmic accountability into the administrative state—*before* harm occurs.

Legislative Developments

In April 2022, Canada introduced the "Digital Charter Implementation Act" (Bill C-27) (5), which includes provisions related to AI and automated decision-making. The Act aims to enhance digital privacy and data protection and establish clear rules for AI use. It is currently under review in Parliament.

Canadian AI Advisory Council

Canada has established advisory councils and working groups to provide guidance on AI policy and regulation, helping to shape the country's approach to AI governance.

While Canada has made significant strides in developing AI-related policies and ethical guidelines, it does not yet have a single, comprehensive piece of legislation equivalent to the EU AI Act. The regulatory landscape is evolving, and ongoing efforts may lead to more detailed and sector-specific regulations in the future.

CHAPTER 11 REFERENCES

1. Pan-Canadian Artificial Intelligence Strategy. Government of Canada. https://ised-isde.canada.ca/site/ai-strategy/en
2. The Personal Information Protection and Electronic Documents Act (PIPEDA). Office of the Privacy Commissioner of Canada. https://www.priv.gc.ca/en/privacy-topics/privacy-laws-in-canada/the-personal-information-protection-and-electronic-documents-act-pipeda/
3. Directive on Automated Decision-Making. 2021. Government of Canada. https://www.tbs-sct.canada.ca/pol/doc-eng.aspx?id=32592
4. A Culture of Ethical AI. Johnny Kung. Canadian Institute for Advanced Research (CIFAR). https://cifar.ca/cifarnews/2021/03/25/a-culture-of-ethical-ai/

5. C-27 an Act to enact the Consumer Privacy Protection Act, the Personal Information and Data Protection Tribunal Act and the Artificial Intelligence and Data Act and to make consequential and related amendments to other Acts. Parliament of Canada. House of Commons. https://www.parl.ca/DocumentViewer/en/44-1/bill/C-27/first-reading

CHAPTER 12

JAPAN

Japan is currently taking a light-touch approach to AI regulation, focusing on guidelines and voluntary compliance rather than strict laws. Although Japan's approach focuses on ensuring that AI systems are used responsibly and ethically, it's approach contrasts with stricter AI regulations in the EU, instead favoring industry-led governance. Current AI Policies in Japan include:

A. **AI Guidelines for Business** (Ver. 1.0): Issued by the Ministry of Economy, Trade and Industry (METI) in April 2024, providing non-binding guidance for AI development and use (1).

B. **Basic Law for the Promotion of Responsible AI** (Draft): Proposed in February 2024, aiming to regulate high-performance AI models while balancing innovation and risk management (1).

C. **Interim Report on AI Policy**: Released by the Japanese Cabinet Office in February 2025, signaling a shift toward lighter AI regulation rather than strict enforcement (2).

While Japan's regulations and guidelines focus on ethical use and principles, they do not have a single comprehensive piece of legislation like the EU AI Act. Instead, Japan's approach is more fragmented but aims to address various aspects of AI governance and ethics through multiple documents and strategies. There have been discussions about introducing enforceable laws targeting foundational AI models. The following are some key aspects of Japan's AI regulation.

AI Strategy

In 2019, Japan released the "AI Strategy 2019" and the "AI Principles" which outline the country's approach to AI development and use. These principles emphasize transparency, accountability, and fairness in AI systems (3). Other aspects of the "AI Strategy2019" include:

A. **AI Utilization**: In 2020, the Japanese government issued the "AI Utilization Guidelines." These guidelines promote the use of AI while ensuring that it is developed and used in ways that are ethical, trustworthy, and transparent. The guidelines include principles related to safety, privacy, and the ethical implications of AI (4).

B. **AI Governance**: In 2021, the Japanese government also introduced the "AI Governance Guidelines", which provide a framework for addressing issues such as transparency, accountability, and fairness in AI systems. These guidelines are intended to support both the public and private sectors in deploying AI responsibly (5).

C. **International Collaboration**: Japan is also involved in international discussions and collaborations on AI ethics and regulation, contributing to global standards and frameworks. They have said a risk-based approach is important.

CHAPTER 12 REFERENCES

1. Fujikouge, T., Kosuge, N. and Matsumoto, F. 2024. Understanding AI Regulations in Japan. DLA Piper. https://www.dlapiper.com/en/insights/publications/2024/10/understanding-ai-regulations-in-japan-current-status-and-future-prospects
2. Habuka, H. 2025. New Government Policy Shows Japan Favors a Light Touch for AI Regulation. Center for Strategic and International Studies. https://www.csis.org/analysis/new-government-policy-shows-japan-favors-light-touch-ai-regulation
3. Integrated Innovation Strategy Promotion Council Decision. AI Strategy 2019 Translation. https://www8.cao.go.jp/cstp/ai/aistratagy2019en.pdf
4. The Conference toward AI Network Society. 2019. AI Utilization Guidelines. Appendix. Translation. https://www.soumu.go.jp/main_content/000658284.pdf

5. Japanese Ministry of Economy, Trade and Industry. 2021.AI Governance in Japan Ver. 1.1—REPORT FROM THE EXPERT GROUP ON HOW AI PRINCIPLES SHOULD BE IMPLEMENTED. https://www.meti.go.jp/shingikai/mono_info_service/ai_shakai_jisso/pdf/20210709_8.pdf

CHAPTER 13

THE NETHERLANDS

Like Australia and the UK, the Netherlands regulations and policies are in response to an algorithmic disaster. At least 3,532 children were taken from their families as a result of financial turmoil triggered when The Dutch tax authority falsely accusing thousands of families of fraud. Following the scandal, The Netherlands has been working to strengthen oversight of AI and algorithms following the Dutch childcare benefits scandal, aiming to prevent discriminatory and incorrect algorithmic decisions. Notably, their efforts include some topics not yet addressed in other countries such as AI literacy and AI Risk Reports.

AI Literacy: Part of the comprehensive plan for AI is Educating the public about AI and algorithmic decision making (1). The government provides a National AI Online Course for civil servants and the general public to create a more widespread understanding of AI's impact. NOLAI (National Education Lab AI) is a government-funded initiative focused on AI in primary, secondary, and special needs education (2).

AI Risk Reports: AI & Algorithmic Risks Report Netherlands (the AP) publishes periodic reports highlighting AI risks, discrimination, and privacy concerns, recommending better risk management and incident monitoring (3).

Although the Dutch do not plan to have their own AI Act, they are fully implementing the EU AI Act. Namely: a) categorizing AI systems by risk level, with strict rules for high-risk AI applications and b) social scoring and manipulative AI are prohibited (4). The Act will be implemented in phases and will be fully in force by August 2nd, 2027. Since February 2nd, 2025, a number of AI systems have been prohibited (those categorized as High-Risk AI, Unacceptable/Prohibited AI and Limited Risk) and organisations that develop or use AI systems have to ensure that their employees are educated about these systems.

CHAPTER 13 REFERENCES

1. Nederlands AI Strategy Report. 2019. European Commission. https://ai-watch.ec.europa.eu/countries/netherlands/netherlands-ai-strategy-report_en
2. National Education Lab. Radboud Universiteit. https://www.ru.nl/en/nolai
3. Dutch Data Protection Authority. Report winter 2023/2024. Department For The Coordination Of Algorithmic Oversight (DCA). https://www.autoriteitpersoonsgegevens.nl/uploads/2024-01/AI & Algorithmic Risks Report Netherlands—winter 2023 2024.pdf
4. EU AI Act. https://www.autoriteitpersoonsgegevens.nl/en/themes/algorithms-ai/eu-ai-act

CHAPTER 14

UNITED KINGDOM

The United Kingdom (UK) investments and innovations are on track to make it an AI superpower. One of the most unusual approaches they have to regulations and innovative technologies is the use of an AI AIRLOCK, which allows it to test technologies and regulations, prior to a full release. In general, it is taking a pro-innovation, principles-based approach to AI regulation, focusing on guidance and sector-specific oversight rather than a single AI law.

Current AI Regulatory Framework

Key elements of the current regulatory framework in the UK are:

A. **AI Regulation White Paper** (March 2023) This outlines five key principles for AI governance: safety, transparency, fairness, accountability, and contestability (1).

B. **Regulators' Strategic Approaches to AI** (May 2024) UK regulators, including the Competition and Markets Authority (CMA), Financial Conduct Authority (FCA), and Information Commissioner's Office (ICO), are integrating AI oversight into their existing frameworks (2).

C. **Artificial Intelligence (Regulation) Bill** (March 2025) Also known as "the AI bill". A private member's bill proposing a statutory AI authority and codified AI governance principles. It reflects growing pressure for formal AI oversight, but it is not yet law (3).

EU AI Act Developments in the UK

The current United Kingdom does not have a regulatory framework for artificial intelligence (AI) that is directly equivalent to the EU AI Act. However, the UK has been developing its own approach to AI regulation and ethical guidelines. An overview of the relevant developments in the UK follow.

A. **AI Strategy and Policy**: The UK Government's "National AI Strategy" was launched in 2021, outlining the country's vision to become a global leader in AI. The strategy focuses on promoting AI innovation, ensuring that AI technologies are used responsibly, and supporting research and development (4).

B. **AI and Data Protection**: The UK's data protection regulations, including the "UK General Data Protection Regulation (UK GDPR)" and the "Data Protection Act 2018", are crucial for AI systems handling personal data. These regulations ensure that personal data is processed transparently and with respect for privacy rights (5,6).

C. **AI Ethics and Guidelines**: The UK issued several documents related to AI ethics and governance. For instance, the "Ethics Guidelines for Trustworthy AI" from the Centre for Data Ethics and Innovation (CDEI) emphasize principles such as transparency, accountability, and fairness in AI systems. The CDEI was restructured in 2024, becoming the Responsible Technology Adoption Unit (RTA) within the Department for Science, Innovation and Technology (DSIT), and as of January 2025, the RTA is no longer a standalone unit and its functions are embedded in other relevant teams in the DSIT, including the Government Digital Service (7).

D. **AI Regulatory Approach**: The UK Government has indicated an interest in developing a more specific regulatory framework for AI.

In April 2024, the UK Government released a "Proposals for AI Regulation" document, which outlines a potential approach to AI regulation. This document suggests a framework focusing on risk-based regulation and emphasizes a principles-based approach rather than a detailed regulatory regime like the EU AI Act (8).

E. **Office for Artificial Intelligence**: The Office for Artificial Intelligence was a UK government body responsible for AI policy and strategy, but in February 2024, it was merged into the AI Policy Directorate within the Department for Science, Innovation and Technology (DSIT). The Office for Artificial Intelligence's former roles included: overseeing and developing policies related to AI, ensure that AI contributes positively to society and addressing potential risks and ethical concerns.

F. **AI Energy Council**: Created in response to in AI Opportunities Action Plan by Command of His Majesty, to address increasing demand for energy with AI innovation, AI Energy Council brings together expert insights on the energy demands of AI (9).

G. **AI AIRLOCK**: The UK established an "AI Regulatory Sandbox" for AI, allowing businesses to test and innovate with AI technologies in a controlled environment. This initiative helps in understanding the practical implications of AI technologies and regulatory approaches (10).

CHAPTER 14 REFERENCES

1. United Kingdom Government (uk.gov). 2022. Implementing the UK's AI regulatory principles: initial guidance for regulators. Department for Science, Innovation and Technology. https://www.gov.uk/government/publications/implementing-the-uks-ai-regulatory-principles-initial-guidance-for-regulators/implementing-the-uks-ai-regulatory-principles-initial-guidance-for-regulators
2. United Kingdom Government (uk.gov) 2024. Regulator's strategic approaches to AI. Department for Science, Innovation and Technology. https://www.gov.uk/government/publications/regulators-strategic-approaches-to-ai/regulators-strategic-approaches-to-ai

3. United Kingdom House of Parliament. 2025. The Artificial Intelligence (Regulation) Bill [HL] (2025). https://kennedyslaw.com/en/thought-leadership/article/2025/the-artificial-intelligence-regulation-bill-closing-the-uks-ai-regulation-gap/
4. UK.GOV 2022. National AI Strategy. Department for Science, Innovation and Technology, Office for Artificial Intelligence, Department for Digital, Culture, Media & Sport and Department for Business, Energy & Industrial Strategy. https://www.gov.uk/government/publications/national-ai-strategy?pStoreID=bizclubsilverb/gb-en/shop
5. Legislation UK.GOV. 2018. Data Protection Act. https://www.legislation.gov.uk/ukpga/2018/12/contents
6. Information Commissioner's Office. UK GDPR guidance and resources. https://ico.org.uk/for-organisations/uk-gdpr-guidance-and-resources/
7. UK.GOV 2021. Centre for Data Ethics and Innovation publishes world first roadmap to catalyse development of AI assurance ecosystem. https://www.gov.uk/government/news/centre-for-data-ethics-and-innovation-publishes-world-first-roadmap-to-catalyse-development-of-ai-assurance-ecosystem
8. UK.GOV. 2024. Implementing the UK's AI regulatory principles: initial guidance for regulators. Department for Science, Innovation and Technology. https://www.gov.uk/government/publications/implementing-the-uks-ai-regulatory-principles-initial-guidance-for-regulators/implementing-the-uks-ai-regulatory-principles-initial-guidance-for-regulators
9. Command of His Majesty. 2025. AI Opportunities Action Plan. Department for Science, Innovation and Technology. ISBN 978-1-5286-5362-6. https://www.gov.uk/government/publications/ai-opportunities-action-plan/ai-opportunities-action-plan
10. UK.GOV 2023. MHRA to launch the AI-Airlock, a new regulatory sandbox for AI developers. Medicines and Healthcare products Regulatory Agency. https://www.gov.uk/government/news/mhra-to-launch-the-ai-airlock-a-new-regulatory-sandbox-for-ai-developers

CHAPTER 15

THE UNITED STATES

Currently the United States does not have a comprehensive federal regulation specifically focused on artificial intelligence (AI). It has no federal policies akin to the EU AI Act or the GDPR. It has, in fact, a deregulatory approach and has recently rolled back much of its previous policies, leaving regulation up to the individual states. In particular, it reversed Biden Executive Order 14110 which focused on ensuring the safe and trust-worthy development of AI through risk mitigation and regulatory oversight. There has been various initiatives, regulations, and guidelines at both the state and city level that address aspects of AI and data privacy. The chapter is divided into data privacy and protection and AI ethics and guidelines. The focus is primarily on the current regulation efforts by individual states, including data privacy and AI regulations.

Data Privacy and Protection

While the US has no comprehensive federal data privacy law, it does have sector-specific laws like the Privacy Act of 1974, HIPAA (Health Insurance Portability and Accountability Act), COPPA (Children's Online Privacy Protection Act), and GLBA (The Gramm-Leach-Bliley Act also known as the Financial Services Modernization Act of 1999, a U.S. federal law that regulates how financial institutions handle customers' personal financial information, requiring them to explain their information-sharing practices and protect sensitive data). The remainder of this section focuses on activities of individual states.

California (1) The first state to pass a Data Privacy and Protection regulation: California Consumer Privacy Act (CCPA) and California Privacy Rights Act (CPRA). These state laws address data privacy and can impact AI systems that handle personal data. The CCPA and its amendment, the CPRA, grant Californians rights such as accessing, deleting, and opting out of the sale of their personal data.

Virginia (2) has a comprehensive privacy law called the Virginia Consumer Data Protection Act (VCDPA), SB 1392, which went into effect on January 1, 2023. Virginia's privacy law is less strict than California's CCPA/CPRA but aligns with GDPR principles, particularly in its controller-processor framework. It grants Virginia residents rights over their personal data and imposes obligations on businesses that process consumer information. Failure to remedy a violation within 30 days can be up to $7,500 each.

Colorado (3) has a comprehensive data privacy law called the Colorado Privacy Act (CPA), SB21-190, which went into effect on July 1, 2023. It grants Colorado residents rights over their personal data and imposes obligations on businesses that process consumer information. Coloradans can access, correct, delete, and opt out of the sale or processing of their personal data..

Connecticut (4) Senate Bill 6: An Act Concerning Personal Data Privacy and Online Monitoring (also known as The Connecticut Data Privacy Act or "CTDPA"), which took effect on July 1, 2023. It grants Connecticut residents rights over their personal data and imposes obligations on businesses that process consumer information. As of January 1, 2025, businesses covered under the CTDPA must honor universal opt out preference signals sent by Connecticut residents.

These laws vary in scope and enforcement, creating an increasing amount of protection.

AI Ethics and Guidelines

In this section we cover some of the efforts in developing AI Ethics and Guidelines happening at the state level. It also includes a special call out for New York City, which has been ahead in AI transparency (for employment) .

California has been at the forefront of AI regulation at the state level. In addition to the CCPA (California Consumer Privacy Act) and CPRA (California Privacy Rights Act) there have been a number of efforts:

A. **Deep fakes**—State bill AB 2655 was passed in September, 2024 to combat AI generated deep fake election and sexual content (5).

B. **Transparency in Healthcare**—State bill AB 3030, also passed in September 2024, requires healthcare providers to disclose the use of generative AI in patient communications and imposes conditions on insurance companies using AI for coverage decisions (6).

C. **Insurance regulation**—SB 1120, passed in January of 2025, establishes specific requirements for how health care service plans and disability insurers in the state may use artificial intelligence, algorithms, or other software tools for utilization review or management (7).

D. **Other**—The state has also introduced bills aimed at increasing transparency and accountability in AI, such as those addressing automated decision-making and facial recognition.

New York City In 2020, New York City introduced regulations requiring companies to be transparent about using Automated Employment Decision Tools (AEDT): "Local Law 144" (8). These regulations require employers to conduct audits on AI systems used in hiring processes to ensure they are fair and non-discriminatory. Effective in December 2021, the evaluation of this approach is mixed—some companies simply ignored it (9).

New York State has introduced the Artificial Intelligence Act (AB 768), a work-in-progress piece of legislation currently under review in the Senate (10). While still far from being enacted, the bill acknowledges a critical reality: AI technologies are already embedded in the lives of New Yorkers, often without public awareness, oversight, or transparency. In this sense, New York is ahead of many other states. It is one of the few jurisdictions to formally recognize —through legislation—that we are the first generation to create machines capable of making decisions about people, and that existing laws do not adequately address this profound shift. More bills:

A. **Restricted Govt. Use**—New York State law (NY A-09430B/S-07543-B) limits the use of AI tools by state agencies. Under the law, government agencies are prohibited from using or procuring automated decision-making systems for functions related to public assistance, that impact civil liberties, safety, or welfare, or affect provided rights. For other uses of automated decision-making systems, government agencies will need to conduct reviews and publish impact assessments (11).

B. **Bill of Rights**—for citizens of New York State, this proposed bill SB-8209 is in the early stages of making its way through the Senate process. It serves as an amendment to New York's existing state technology law. From the bill: "any New York resident affected by any system making decisions without human intervention be entitled to certain rights and protections to ensure that the system impacting their lives do so lawfully, properly, and with meaningful oversight" (12).

Colorado: the first state to enact a *comprehensive* law relating to artificial intelligence (AI) systems: CAIA—The Colorado Artificial Intelligence Act or SB24-205. Expected to take effect February 1, 2026. Modeled after the EU AI Act, it shares a risk-based approach to AI regulation (13).

Washington The state is home to Microsoft and Open AI, the heart of generative AI innovation. The state attorney's office is quite active in developing AI-legislation:

A. **AI Detection Tools**—House Bill 1170 requires providers of generative AI to make an AI detection tool freely available to users for identifying AI-generated content, covering images, videos, and audio (14).

B. **AI in Political Ads**—A bill passed in 2023 requires disclosure if audio or images in political advertisements are manipulated. SB 5152—2023-24 relates to bill 1170 (above) but zeroes in on political campaigns (15).

C. **Schools**—The Washington State Office of Superintendent of Public Instruction (OSPI) offers guidance for schools on integrating AI-assisted technologies, emphasizing data privacy and ethical considerations (16).

D. **AI Task Force**—The Washington State Attorney General's Office established an AI Task Force to assess current AI uses and trends, and make recommendations for potential legislation. This task force will convene various stakeholders to discuss AI's benefits and challenges. Their report from 2024 can be accessed at (17).

Utah: The UAIPA, Utah's AI Policy Act, SB 149, became effective May 1, 2024. It focuses on consumer protection and transparency regarding the use of generative AI systems and has a policy for enforcement. For example, businesses must disclose the use of generative AI if a consumer asks or prompts them to do so. Violations of the UAIPA can result in civil penalties of up to $2,500 per violation, and the Utah Department of Consumer Protections can bring actions in court to enforce the law (18).

The Elvis Act and Other Developments

These are but a few of the states developing regulations. Tennessee, for example, has created "the ELVIS Act"—Ensuring Likeness Voice and Image Security (ELVIS) Act in March 2024. This legislation was the first in the U.S. to regulate AI-generated audio deepfakes and voice cloning, specifically protecting musicians from the unauthorized use of their voices. However, many states have still not enacted significant AI legislation or established task forces. This is likely to change as the AI landscape is rapidly evolving, and in upcoming legislative sessions more states are expected to introduce AI-related bills.

While the U.S. lacks a unified federal AI regulatory framework, these various initiatives and guidelines are slowly shaping a patchwork of AI governance. Some states, such as Colorado are taking a comprehensive approach modeling their policies along the lines of the EU AI Act, while others, such as New York, are modeling their regulations along the lines of a Bill of Rights. The regulatory environment is evolving rapidly, and more comprehensive federal regulations may emerge in the future as AI technology and its impacts continue to develop. For the most recent updates, it's useful to follow developments from relevant government agencies and legislative bodies.

CHAPTER 15 REFERENCES

1. California Office of the Attorney General. 2018. California Consumer Privacy Act of 2018 (CCPA). https://oag.ca.gov/privacy/ccpa
2. Virginia Government. 2023. The Virginia Consumer Data Protection Act (VCDPA) SB 1392. Virginia's Legislative Information System. https://legacylis.virginia.gov/cgi-bin/legp604.exe?211+sum+SB1392
3. Colorado General Assembly. Protect Personal Data Privacy SB21-190. https://leg.colorado.gov/bills/sb21-190

4. CT.GOV 2022.Senate Bill 6: An Act Concerning Personal Data Privacy and Online Monitoring (also known as The Connecticut Data Privacy Act or "CTDPA"). https://portal.ct.gov/ag/sections/privacy/the-connecticut-data-privacy-act
5. California Legislative Information. 2024. AB-2655 Defending Democracy from Deepfake Deception Act of 2024. https://leginfo.legislature.ca.gov/faces/billNavClient.xhtml?bill_id=202320240AB2655
6. California Legislative Information. 2024. AB-3030 Health care services: artificial intelligence. https://leginfo.legislature.ca.gov/faces/billTextClient.xhtml?bill_id=202320240AB3030
7. California Legislative Information. 2024. Health care coverage: utilization review. https://leginfo.legislature.ca.gov/faces/billNavClient.xhtml?bill_id=202320240SB1120
8. New York City Council. 2021. 2021/144 A local law to amend the administrative code of the city of New York, in relation to automated employment decision tools. https://legistar.council.nyc.gov/LegislationDetail.aspx?ID=4344524&GUID=B051915D-A9AC-451E-81F8-6596032FA3F9
9. Ottaway, A. 2024. Everyone Ignores' New York City's Workplace AI Law. *Law360.* https://www.law360.com/employment-authority/articles/1808951#
10. New York State Assembly. 2025. AB-A768:New York artificial intelligence consumer protection act. *The New York State Senate.* https://www.nysenate.gov/legislation/bills/2025/A768
11. New York State Assembly. 2024. A09430B Oversight of automated decision-making in government act. https://assembly.state.ny.us/leg/?bn=A09430&term=2023&Summary=Y&Actions=Y
12. New York State Senate. 2024. The New York artificial intelligence bill of rights. https://legislation.nysenate.gov/pdf/bills/2023/S8209
13. Legislation of Colorado Government. 2024. SB24-205 Concerning consumer protections in interactions with Artificial Intelligence systems. *General Assembly of the State of Colorado.* https://leg.colorado.gov/sites/default/files/2024a_205_signed.pdf
14. Washington State Legislature. 2025. HB 1170—2025-26. Informing users when content is developed or modified by artificial intelligence. https://app.leg.wa.gov/billsummary?BillNumber=1170&Initiative=false&Year=2025
15. Washington State Legislature. 2023. SB 5152—2023-24. Defining synthetic media in campaigns for elective office, and providing relief for candidates and campaigns. https://app.leg.wa.gov/billsummary?BillNumber=5152&Year=2023&Initiative=false
16. Washington Office of the Superintendent. 2025. *Human-Centered Artificial Intelligence in Schools.* https://ospi.k12.wa.us/student-success/resources-subject-area/human-centered-artificial-intelligence-schools
17. Washington State AI Task Force. 2024. Inaugural Report of the Washington State Artificial Intelligence Task Force. *Washington State Attorney General's Office.*
18. Utah State Legislature. 2024. Artificial Intelligence Policy Act. https://le.utah.gov/~2024/bills/static/SB0149.html

CHAPTER 16

SINGAPORE

Voluntary Framework Singapore released the Model AI Governance Framework in 2019, with a second edition in 2020 (1). *It's not a law,* but a voluntary, practical guide designed to help organizations deploy AI responsibly, especially in high-stakes sectors like finance, healthcare, and public services. The framework is structured around two foundational principles:

1. *AI Should Be Explainable, Transparent, and Fair:* Organizations should provide *meaningful explanations* for AI-assisted decisions, especially when they affect individuals' rights. There should be clear internal policies about how data is used, how models are trained, and what safeguards are in place.

2. *AI Should Be Human-Centric*: Humans must remain in control and be able to intervene when necessary. Systems should be tested for unintended bias and evaluated for impact on individuals and communities.

The framework includes concrete guidance on:

A. Internal governance structures (like setting up AI ethics boards).

B. Risk-based decision-making (more scrutiny for higher-impact AI).

C. Operations management (monitoring models over time).

D. Customer relationship management (offering redress, transparency).

In general, their approach is focused on real-world deployment and commercial contexts and is expected to be helpful for small companies, tech giants or governments.

In our opinion, the key word here is "should". When a framework like Singapore's says "offer redress," it's calling for systems that not only make decisions, but can also listen, learn, and fix themselves when they get it wrong. This was one of the major failures in Robodebt: many people tried to appeal, but the system was confusing, slow, and stacked against them, with no effective remedy until a massive lawsuit and Royal Commission forced it.

The voluntary approach may be successful in countries where their culture highly prizes its people for characteristics of ethics, integrity and honor. In the U.S. and other places, where money is the key to success and where crime and corruption are increasing, this would not work. If a framework is not legally binding bad actors can and do exploit the system, taking advantage of loopholes, etc. A hybrid volunteer-legal framework could be the answer. This may be especially important when oversight is removed (e.g. when Microsoft and Google removed their AI ethics groups and when the U.S. government removed not only oversight but existing policy).

CHAPTER 16 REFERENCES

1. Model AI Governance Framework Second Edition. 2020. Personal Data Protection Commission Singapore. https://www.pdpc.gov.sg/-/media/files/pdpc/pdf-files/resource-for-organisation/ai/sgmodelaigovframework2.pdf

APPENDIX

AI CREATES THE LAW

APPENDIX—AI CREATES THE LAW

While the previous chapters have focused on the laws being written by people, this appendix covers law from a different angle: law being crafted and practiced by Artificial Intelligence (AI) systems. This "governing-by-algorithm" again takes us into into unknown territories. We cover this development as it is happening in the United Arab Emirates (UAE) and China.

New Developments, Issues and Considerations. While AI has primarily assisted lawyers and court officials until now, it is increasingly being used to draft legislation, assess its societal impact, and even preside over virtual courtrooms as "smart judges" capable of issuing legally binding decisions. This shift toward algorithmic governance raises significant legal and ethical concerns that must be addressed before widespread adoption. Nevertheless, some countries are already moving forward.

Specific examples of how AI is useful for law include: research (e-discovery and evidence analysis), litigation support (case management, litigation prediction) and risk assessment (compliance) tools. Judicial decision-support systems are also used, including for making sentencing recommendations and for parole eligibility determination and prediction (i.e., propensity to re-offend). But some countries are taking a more encompassing approach to integrating AI into their legal systems. For example, China has deployed AI-driven "smart judges" designed for virtual, internet courts intended to automate small claims legal processes. And recently, the UAE announced it will integrate AI into its overall lawmaking processes to streamline its legislative efforts.

China's Smart Courts

China's virtual internet courts offer a vivid example of the potential of integrating AI technology into a judicial system. Typically referred to as "smart courts," these systems are designed to handle Internet-related issues around e-commerce, IP rights, and online financial disputes. First introduced in 2017 in the tech-hub city of Hangzhou, China has now expanded smart courts to other cities, including Beijing and Guangzhou (1).

Through the innovative use of AI, blockchain and other digital technologies, smart courts are designed to enhance the efficiency, accessibility, and transparency of the legal process: litigants can file cases, present evidence, and participate in hearings entirely online. To ensure the integrity of evidence and other legal information, blockchain serves to verify, timestamp and maintain submitted documents. This helps reduce risks around tampering and fraud (2).

The most impressive aspect of smart courts is their "smart judges," which use AI to assist with case management, evidence analysis, and even to generate recommendations based on legal precedents. Other online dispute resolution tools provide additional means for parties to resolve legal disputes without having to resort to [physical] court appearances. All of these features help speed-up case resolution.

China's internet courts demonstrate the potential benefits that can be gained from integrating AI into governance, serving as a global example of innovation in the legal system. Smart courts automate and streamline the legal process, providing benefits around time savings and legal resources. This is especially beneficial to a country with such a massive population and high volume of court cases. That said, it's important to note, that many AI systems in the U.S., especially those that are model-based (deep learning/generative AI) have struggled to overcome faulty decision making due to bias, hallucinations, and so on. The details of China's code are not widely known, so it is possible they have solved those issues. Although AI provides the intelligence behind China's smart courts and smart judges, ultimately human judges still retain overall authority and have the last say with verdicts and other decisions (3).

While these developments are in the early stages, it is a promising direction for a country with such a large population. The backlog for court cases can run several years.

The UAE's Regulatory Intelligence System

The UAE's plans for AI and the law take us even further into the future. They are using AI to develop a new Regulatory Intelligence System (RIS) that will help create and maintain the country's laws. This initiative, approved in April 2025 by the UAE Cabinet, aims to integrate AI into lawmaking in an effort to accelerate legislative reform by enhancing the efficiency, accuracy, and responsiveness of the country's legislative processes. Again, we have no way of knowing how well they have managed to measure or reduce the kinds of errors that are being experienced with AI technologies in U.S. systems.

UAE Prime Minister, Sheikh Mohammed bin Rashid Al Maktoum announced the decision to build the system in several posts on X (formerly Twitter). His post basically described how the UAE will make extensive use of AI for creating new laws and monitoring their impact on the country at the national and local levels. Here is the post from X (Twitter): "Today, I chaired the Cabinet meeting at Qasr Al Watan in Abu Dhabi, where we made key decisions to advance legislative processes. We approved the establishment of the Regulatory Intelligence Office within the Cabinet. This office will work on creating a comprehensive legislative plan that brings together all federal and local laws in the UAE, connecting them through artificial intelligence with judicial rulings, executive procedures, and public services. The new system will allow us to track the daily impact of laws on our people and economy using large-scale data, and it will regularly suggest updates to our legislation. The system will be linked to leading global research centers to follow the best international policies and legislative practices, tailoring them to fit the UAE's unique context" (4).

Here's what we currently know about the RIS. It will employ an AI-powered "legislative mapping" capability to generate a centralized map that links all UAE federal and local laws with judicial rulings, executive procedures, and public services. Key functionality includes the ability to perform real-time impact analysis—including tracking the daily effects of laws on UAE society and the economy, and recommending updates to the law as determined via big data analysis. Exactly what will be measured, and how, is not clear. The system will also issue findings directly to lawmakers, with the AI-driven approach expected to help reduce legislative drafting time by up to 70% (5).

The RIS will take a global perspective to lawmaking: it will connect UAE laws with leading global research centers. The goal: align UAE laws with international standards while at the same time maintaining local relevance; this includes continuously monitoring global legislative trends, identifying gaps and inconsistencies within UAE laws, and suggesting reforms (6).

According to the PM, "This new legislative system, powered by artificial intelligence, will change how we create laws, making the process faster and more precise. It will ensure that our legislative framework stands out, aligning our laws with the best global practices while staying true to the unique path of our rapid development" (7,8).

Building the System The RIS marks a significant development in AI-driven governance, making the UAE one of the first to adopt such an encompassing, data-driven, adaptive legal framework. Of course, the system still needs to get built. To facilitate implementation, the UAE has established a new agency to oversee the project: the Regulatory Intelligence Office (RIO). The UAE is no stranger to AI. Its "National

Strategy for AI 2031" aims to integrate the technology across various economic sectors (9). It's Ministry of Justice has already deployed several AI legal tools, including a virtual legal advisor and family law bot (10).

Issues and Considerations with Using AI in Legal Processes Despite its potential to enhance accessibility, efficiency, and accuracy, applying AI in legal domains presents a number of issues and considerations.

Bias Building AI systems requires huge amounts of data for model training and testing. This typically involves historical data, meaning there is the risk that the AI models and algorithms used in legal systems could learn existing prejudices pertaining to race, sex, gender, age, socioeconomic and other biases. Consequently, all data used for training and testing purposes should be thoroughly vetted to weed out biases to prevent AI legal systems from generating decisions or outcomes that could reflect existing biases or inequalities.

Transparency and Accountability The biggest drawback with AI technology remains its inability to provide a good explanation. This is particularly true of systems employing deep learning neural networks. Consequently, lack of transparency in AI legal systems is a serious issue because it can undermine public trust and lead to skepticism about the fairness of AI-driven outcomes and even a jurisdiction's legal system in general. Accountability in AI-driven legal systems is complex. When mistakes occur, who should be held responsible—the legal professionals using the system, or the developers who built it? Ensuring transparency and clearly defined accountability is essential to uphold fairness and to maintain public and judicial trust in AI-assisted justice.

Ethical Considerations Ethical considerations with using AI in legal systems are significant. A major concern is the potential for biases that have been "baked-into" AI algorithms. As discussed above, biases can stem from the use of poorly vetted data used to train AI models, and which can inadvertently reflect societal prejudices. As a result, decisions rendered by an AI legal system could unfairly disadvantage certain groups, thereby unintentionally perpetuating racial, socioeconomic or other systemic biases. Concerns around bias, transparency and accountability are frequently cited as one of the leading issues by opponents against the use of AI for legal decision making (11).

Dependence on AI Over Human Judgment While AI can assist in automating legal processes, it should not take precedent over human judgment. There's the danger of the legal system (i.e., overall legal process) becoming too reliant on AI, which could undermine the justice process. Basically, the law is a very complex field requiring human discretion, intuition, judgment, moral understanding and empathy for its application, especially when it comes to weighing the intricacies of complex legal cases requiring the analysis and understanding of human behavior. Consequently, lawmakers should ensure that AI remains a tool rather than the primary decision-maker in legal systems.

Adaptability and Interpretation Laws, and their application in legal cases, often require nuanced interpretation as well as adaptation to the evolving needs of society. AI legal systems may not be able to adapt fast enough (have new models trained) to take into account changing political, cultural, and economic trends in the same way that humans (judges, attorney, etc.) can. Additionally, it may prove difficult to amass sufficient data for training new models.

Taken together, these challenges above underline the need for strong human oversight, ethical guidelines, and transparency when integrating AI into legal processes.

Conclusion AI is rapidly reshaping the legal landscape. While some countries are adopting nuanced approaches to its integration, others are ambitiously incorporating AI into their legal systems to streamline processes and boost efficiency. Innovations range from smart judges presiding over virtual courts to advanced systems capable of drafting laws and assessing their impact on society. In short, these developments signal a transformative era in legal technology.

But alongside these advancements are serious challenges that must be solved—chiefly issues around bias, accountability, transparency, and ethical concerns. Addressing these challenges will require developing comprehensive ethical frameworks, transparent systems, and applying continued human oversight to ensure that AI serves as a tool for justice rather than a source of uncertainty. Ultimately, striking the right balance will be critical in harnessing AI's potential while safeguarding fairness and trust within the legal domain.

Appendix References

1. https://learningenglish.voanews.com/a/robot-justice-the-rise-of-china-s-internet-courts-/5201677.html
2. https://www.lexisnexis.ca/en-ca/ihc/2020-02/robot-justice-chinas-use-of-internet-courts.page
3. https://lexir.co/2024/09/20/chinas-smart-courts-initiative-a-case-study-in-ai-integration
4. Rashid Al Maktoum, M. [@HHShkMod]. n.d. "Today, I chaired the Cabinet meeting at Qasr Al Watan in Abu Dhabi, where we made key decisions to advance legislative processes" [images attached]. X (Formerly Twitter) . Retrieved April 14, 2025.
5. https://www.middleeastainews.com/p/uae-cabinet-new-ai-legal-system
6. https://www.gulftoday.ae/news/2025/04/14/uae-launches-worlds-first-ai-enabled-ecosystem-in-government
7. Cornish, C. 2025. UAE set to use AI to write laws in world first. Financial Times. https://www.ft.com/content/9019cd51-2b55-4175-81a6-eafcf28609c3
8. ODS Team. 2025. UAE to Use AI to Draft and Amend Laws in Global First. Open Data Science. https://opendatascience.com/uae-to-use-ai-to-draft-and-amend-laws-in-global-first/
9. https://ai.gov.ae/strategy/
10. https://www.moj.gov.ae/en/artificial-intelligence.aspx
11. https://aicompetence.org/ai-in-courtrooms-judges-replaced-by-algorithms/

A Word on AI Hype

While there are truly remarkable new AI technologies emerging on the world stage, we must be careful not to let our excitement run amok. Some people tend to impart a magical element to AI, thinking that it can do no wrong. But also there are promises and public statements on what it is capable of, which heightens our expectations. This is known as "AI Hype." When these romantic technical ideals fail to meet our expectations, AI experiences what is called an AI Winter. So it is important, especially now, to ensure these systems work properly, without bias, errors and so on. And that when errors do arise, we LISTEN to the people who are reporting them. To do otherwise would be walking off the cliff into the valley of AI Hype. These laws, together with our own sense of care, infused into our designs, can help us ensure this doesn't happen.

Parting words

This is the end of the book, so we'll leave you with some parting words...but they're not ours. We fed the book into Chat-GPT and asked it to summarize the book. What came back was rather poetic:

In a glass case in the British Library, under low light and cool air, a parchment lies pressed behind ultraviolet-filtered glass. It is smaller than you'd expect, more browned than yellow, and the Latin is not handwritten but crowded together in a dense, blocky script pressed by a scribe in 1215.

The Magna Carta—*the Great Charter*—is often cited and rarely read. Most of its provisions dealt with feudal trivia: fish traps on the Thames, the right of a widow not to remarry, the proper standard for wine. But buried among the wine laws and river customs is a phrase that survived revolutions: *To no one will we sell, to no one deny or delay right or justice.*

Eight centuries later, a software program flagged a benefits recipient in Melbourne for repayment. It did so automatically. There was no hearing. There was no explanation. The program did not know about fish traps or widows or justice. It simply ran.

The Magna Carta was a response to power wielded without restraint. So, too, is the idea of a duty of care for algorithms. The question is whether we will write it before the machine writes it for us.

GLOSSARY

ADOC—ADOC is a proposed framework that aligns algorithms with existing values of common law and the Magna Carta. Inspired by the long-standing legal, ethical and social norm called duty of care, it also proposes embedding ethical responsibility and care directly into algorithmic systems.

Algorithm—A structured set of instructions for solving problems or processing data. Algorithms drive technology, from search engines to AI and video games. They also create models used for automated decision-making and generative AI.

Algorithmification—The broad, fast-moving trend of replacing human processes with algorithmic systems—without adequate oversight or ethical design.

Ban-Evading—When someone who has been banned from a platform or community creates a new account or uses another identity to rejoin and continue harmful or disruptive behavior.

Brigading—When a group of people coordinate online to flood someone's posts, comments, or content—often to harass, intimidate, or manipulate public opinion.

Christchurch Call—An international pledge launched in 2019 after the Christchurch attacks to reduce online terrorist and extremist content, backed by governments and tech companies.

Christchurch Mosque Attacks—A 2019 terrorist shooting at two mosques in Christchurch, New Zealand, that killed 51 people. The attack was livestreamed, raising global concern about online extremism.

Cyberbullying—The use of digital technologies—such as social media, messaging platforms, gaming environments, or email—to harass, threaten, humiliate, coercively control or intimidate another person.

Cyberbullying can include spreading false information, sending abusive messages, sharing private information without consent, or deliberately excluding someone online. Unlike traditional bullying, it can occur at any time and often reaches a wider audience quickly.

Dogpiling—When many people target one individual with negative or hostile comments, often all at once, creating an overwhelming and sometimes frightening online attack.

Doxxing—Publishing someone's private or identifying information online without consent, with the intent to harass, threaten, or cause harm in real life.

Gaslighting—A psychological manipulation tactic where someone makes another person question their own reality, memory, or perceptions, often leading them to feel confused, anxious, or even doubt their sanity.

Global South (Global Southern Region)—The Global South is a term used to broadly describe countries in Africa, Latin America and The Caribbean that are characterized by lower economic development, historical marginalization, and often grappling with the legacy of colonialism.

Grooming—the act of manipulating someone (often a child, female or other vulnerable person) in order to build trust over time, typically with the aim of exploiting, abusing, or manipulating them for some ulterior motive (sexual exploitation, financial fraud, trafficking, etc.).

Horizon IT Postal Scandal—A faulty accounting software used by the UK Post Office that led to one of the biggest miscarriages of justice in British history.

Livestreaming Violence—Broadcasting acts of violence in real time over the internet, often via social media platforms. These streams can rapidly spread graphic content, traumatize viewers, and serve as propaganda or performative acts meant to provoke attention.

Oblivatronix—A term introduced to describe the current generation of indifferent, harm-prone algorithms designed to "do the job" but not to care about or even notice human harm.

Online Extremism—The use of digital platforms to promote, recruit for, or organize around extremist ideologies. This includes hate speech, conspiracy theories, and calls to violence.

Real-World Harm—Examples like Robodebt (Australia), Horizon IT (UK), and Toeslagenaffaire (Netherlands) are used to show the high cost of ignoring duty of care in digital systems.

Robodebt—An unlawful automated debt recovery scheme used by the Australian government from 2016 to 2020.

Sealioning—A form of trolling where someone repeatedly and aggressively asks for evidence or clarification, often in bad faith, in order to derail a conversation or frustrate the person they are engaging with. Sometimes referred to as "sea-lioning."

Swatting—A dangerous hoax where someone falsely reports a serious emergency—like a hostage situation or bomb threat—to send armed police (often a SWAT team) to another person's address, putting them at real physical risk.

Toeslagenaffaire—Also known as the Dutch childcare benefits scandal, this was a major political scandal in the Netherlands where thousands of families were wrongly accused of fraud by the tax authorities. Many were separated from their children. The scandal ultimately led to the resignation of the Dutch government in 2021.

United Nations' Universal Declaration of Human Rights—A landmark document adopted by the UN General Assembly in 1948, outlining fundamental human rights that should be universally protected. It has influenced numerous international treaties and national laws

DISCLAIMER: This area is moving very quickly. This summary is intended to be a helpful but short informal glance at the regulatory progress for algorithms and AI as of May, 2025. It was compiled from searches on government web sites, books, research papers and discussions with colleagues. We found it especially helpful to look at multiple sources and especially original government sources. Co-Pilot was helpful in pointing out some references more quickly, but knowing the hallucinations it (and all generative AI systems) can sometimes have, we used it not for information but to point to possible research sources, looking to our own search results.—clm

About US

Cindy Mason, CMT, Ph.D. is a computer scientist and former Stanford Medicine fellow whose work explores the social, medical and ethical edges of artificial intelligence. She has pioneered a number of "firsts": at NASA Ames she was part of the team to send the first undersea autonomous vehicle to Antarctica; at U.C. Berkeley she created the first software agent programming language to represent and input sensory measurements of emotion. With roots in both computer science and human science, she has published widely on intelligent agents and psychophysiology and has pioneered the new field of Artificial Compassion, causing some to call her the "mother of Artificial Compassion" in machine design. A key contributor to the NYT bestseller *How to Create a Mind* and author of *The Emotion Organon,* Cindy bridges worlds—AI, human sciences, and society. She also hosts an AI literacy podcast for the public called RADIO AI, featuring conversations with the people inventing our algorithmic future.

Curt Hall is a seasoned tech analyst, researcher, and editor who's been tracking the front lines of digital innovation for over two decades. His work dives deep into AI, machine learning, NLP, big data, and the systems shaping how we live and decide. A longtime contributor to the Cutter Consortium (an Arthur D. Little Community) and editor of multiple tech strategy journals, Curt brings sharp insight and a grounded perspective to the fast-moving world of algorithmic systems and digital ethics. He can be contacted on LinkedIn.

Other books by Cindy Mason include
Artificial Intelligence and the Environment ISBN 9781733524803
The Emotion Organon ISBN 9798851933400

Other books by Curt Hall include:
Intelligent Software Systems Development. ISBN 9780471592440

www.ingramcontent.com/pod-product-compliance
Lightning Source LLC
LaVergne TN
LVHW022051200926
848481LV00003B/861
9798990475014